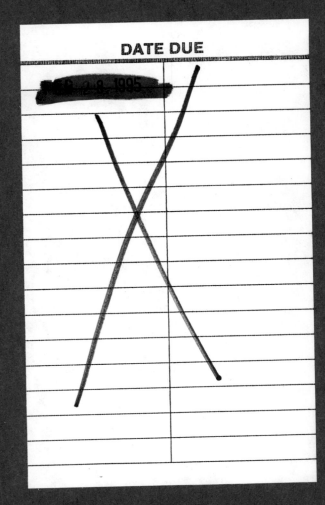

Nietzsche: A Self-Portrait from His Letters

Friedrich Nietzsche

Nietzsche *A Self-Portrait from His Letters*

Edited and translated by
Peter Fuss and Henry Shapiro

Harvard University Press
Cambridge, Massachusetts
1971

© 1971 by the President and Fellows of Harvard College
All Rights Reserved
Distributed in Great Britain by Oxford University Press, London
Library of Congress Catalog Card Number 73-134953
SBN 674-62425-4
Printed in the United States of America

In Memory of Philip Wheelwright

"I should have mentioned Walter Scott
along with milk and sleep"

Preface

This book tells the story of Nietzsche's life, and the narrator is Nietzsche himself. It is obviously not a complete story, nor does it have the fullness of a traditional biography or scholarly study. Something – a good deal – had to give way when the demands of well-roundedness and balance met those of economy and clarity of development. We reached two decisions that are a bit unusual. In the first place, our selection of letters begins when Nietzsche is already twenty-one. With very few exceptions, his earlier letters are of little interest; in most respects Nietzsche matured quite late. And second, we leave out not only the less important *letters,* but the less interesting *portions* of the letters we do use.

Since this is essentially Nietzsche's story and not that of his correspondents, the letters, as we have pruned them, may leave the reader with an exaggerated sense (if that is possible) of Nietzsche's egocentrism. He did have a very real capacity to devote himself to the problems of others. We hope we have allowed it to show through. The chronology and the biographical sketches that follow the text should help to correct the misleading impression, which Nietzsche himself fostered, that during his last functional decade he was a hermit.

Translation was of course our major problem. We wanted to try our hand at giving readers with little or no German some idea of the beauty, the concreteness, the classical simplicity of Nietzsche's prose style. These carry over best, we believe, when preference is given to the Anglo-Saxon rather than the Latin heritage of our language.

The texts for the letters we have chosen, with several exceptions indicated in the notes, are from the very fine selection in Karl Schlechta's three-volume edition of Nietzsche, published by Carl Hanser Verlag (Munich, 1954–56). Our explanatory notes, like the book as a whole, presuppose only the most casual acquaintance with Nietzsche and his world. We would, however, recommend reading Nietzsche's works alongside his letters, and consulting a biography such as Hollingdale's.

Of all those who listened to or read our translations of these letters at various stages of progress and offered valuable criticism, we must mention in particular Anna Bovell and the late Philip Wheelwright in America, Ulrich Sonnemann and Ludwig Döderlein in Germany. For research assistance we are indebted to Sebastian Frobenius; for clerical assistance, to Kristin Sobotta, Margritta Aulehla, Janiece Fister, and Oscar Morales. Our wives, Carol Fuss and Eleanor Shapiro, gave generous help at every stage. The University of California at Riverside and the University of Missouri at St. Louis assisted us financially. We appreciate the considerable resources placed at our disposal by the Bayerische Staatsbibliothek in Munich.

Peter Fuss
Henry Shapiro

St. Louis, Missouri
June 1970

Contents

Illustrations

The Letters

Abbreviations Used in the Notes (see the bibliography for full citations)

Bernoulli. Carl Albrecht Bernoulli. *Franz Overbeck und Friedrich Nietzsche: eine Freundschaft.*

BGN. Die Briefe Peter Gasts an Friedrich Nietzsche. Edited by A. Mendt.

Biog. Elisabeth Förster-Nietzsche. *Das Leben Friedrich Nietzsches.* (The original, two-volume edition.)

BNO. Nietzsches Briefwechsel mit Franz Overbeck. Edited by Richard Oehler and Carl Albrecht Bernoulli.

Brann. Hellmut Walther Brann: *Nietzsche und die Frauen.*

GBr. Friedrich Nietzsches Gesammelte Briefe. Edited by Elisabeth Förster-Nietzsche *et al.*

HKG Br. Friedrich Nietzsche: Historisch-Kritische Gesamtausgabe der Briefe. Edited by Wilhelm Hoppe and Karl Schlechta.

Schlechta. *Friedrich Nietzsche: Werke in drei Bänden.* Edited by Karl Schlechta.

1 TO CARL VON GERSDORFF

Naumburg, 7 April 1866

Dear friend, once in a while there come those hours of quiet contemplation when, with joy and sadness mixed, we hover over our everyday lives, like those lovely summer days stretching themselves comfortably over the hills, as Emerson describes them so well. It's then, as he says, that nature achieves perfection; and we — we are then free of the curse of our ever watchful will, we are then pure eye, contemplative and disinterested. In this most desirable of moods I'm taking pen in hand to answer your kind letter, which is so full of good ideas. . . .

Three things afford me relief, rare moments of relief from my work: my Schopenhauer, the music of Schumann, and solitary walks. Yesterday a magnificent thunderstorm built up in the sky. I hurried up a nearby hill. . . . The storm broke with tremendous force, gusting and hailing. I felt an incomparable upsurge, and realized that we actually understand nature only when we must fly to her to escape our cares and afflictions. What was man and his restless striving to me then! What was that endless "Thou shalt," "Thou shalt not"! How different the lightning, the wind, the hail — sovereign powers, without ethics! How happy, how strong they are, pure will, unclouded by intellect!

2 TO CARL VON GERSDORFF

[Leipzig, c. 13 July 1866][1]

. . . Never in 50 years have we stood so close to the fulfillment of our German hopes. I'm gradually beginning to comprehend that there really wasn't any other, gentler path than the terrible one of a war to the bitter end. Just a short time ago Corssen's[2] view "that only on Austria's ruins could Germany's future be built" seemed frightfully inflammatory. But so old an edifice as Austria won't crumble so easily. Decrepit as it may be, there will always be "good and true" neighbors to support it; its collapse, after all, could cause damage to their own houses. This, applied to our current situation in Europe, is the Napoleonic doctrine of the balance of power, a balance whose center is supposed to lie in Paris. To that center an Austria in distress appeals for help. And as long as that center is in Paris, nothing will change in Europe as a whole. So our national effort cannot stop short of overthrowing the European order, or at least of making the attempt. Should it fail, I hope we two shall have the honor of falling in battle, struck by French bullets. . . .[3]

[1] The source for this letter is *HKG Br* II, 66–67.

[2] Wilhelm Paul Corssen (1820–1875), philologist and archaeologist. He taught history at Pforta for twenty-two years. Corssen is the only one of Nietzsche's teachers mentioned in the works he published.

[3] A year and a half later, Nietzsche's Prussian sympathies were still ardent. On 16 February 1868, he wrote to Gersdorff: "Bismarck affords me boundless delight. I read his speeches as though I were drinking heady wine" (Schlechta, III, 992).

3 TO CARL VON GERSDORFF

Kösen, 11 October 1866[1]

. . . I'm not traveling this vacation, but sitting in studious seclusion in Kösen, where my mother and I have been living for four weeks in order to avoid the cholera in Naumburg. . . .

. . . Precisely because of its contrast with life in Bonn, I have found this past year of study in Leipzig just delightful. Whereas there I had to submit to silly rules and regulations, amusements were forced on me which I found repugnant, and an idle existence among rather crude people kept me in a very sour mood, in Leipzig everything did an about-face in an unexpected way. Pleasant, kind, friendly relationships, undeserved favor on Ritschl's part, fellow students who share my aspirations, a good landlord and landlady, good concerts, etc., — truly enough to make Leipzig a very pleasant city for me. . . .

. . . We can consider ourselves lucky to have basked in the rays of the setting sun at Pforta. Its period of greatness is all over; the determined effort of several government officials to force Pforta down to the level of other schools has been completely successful. . . .

I've done little music, since I have no piano at my disposal in Kösen. Nevertheless, the piano arrangement of Richard Wagner's *Valkyrie* has accompanied me. My feelings about it are very mixed, so that I dare not pass judgment on it. Some great beauty and power is counterbalanced by equally great ugliness and imperfection. But $+a + (-a)$, according to Riese and Buchbinder, equals 0. . . .

[1] The source for this letter is *HKG Br* II, 94–95, 97–98.

4 TO PAUL DEUSSEN
Naumburg, 4 April 1867
. . . You won't believe how personally I'm bound to Ritschl, so that I neither can nor want to tear myself free. . . . You have no idea how this man cares about and works for every single individual of whom he's fond, how well he knows how to fulfill my desires, which often I hardly dare express, and how free he is of that pedantic arrogance and that wary reserve characteristic of so many scholars. He is very outspoken and impartial, and I know that such natures must often give offense. He is the only man whose criticism I enjoy hearing: all his judgments are so healthy and forceful, so fully attuned to the truth that he acts as a kind of scholarly conscience for me.

So: I'm going to stay near him for a while longer. My prospects for the future are indefinite, consequently quite favorable. For the only terrible thing is certainty. My aspirations lean towards earning a few hundred thalers a year in some honorable and not too time-consuming way, thereby preserving my freedom for a number of years. . . .

5 TO CARL VON GERSDORFF
Naumburg, 6 April 1867
. . . This vacation I want to get my work on the sources of Laertius down on paper; I'm still pretty much in the first

stages. You'll laugh when I confess what troubles me most: my German style (never mind my Latin; once I've come to grips with my mother tongue, foreign languages will have their turn). The scales are falling from my eyes, I've been living all too long in stylistic innocence. The categorical imperative "Thou shalt write" has awakened me. I was trying to do something I haven't tried except at school: to write well—and suddenly the pen in my hand went limp. I couldn't do it; that vexed me. And my ears were ringing with the stylistic precepts of Lessing, Lichtenberg, and Schopenhauer. It always consoled me that these three authorities unanimously insist that it's hard to write well, that no one has a good style by nature, that you really have to work like a dog to get one. I never again want to write in so wooden and dry, so straitlaced and constricted a way as I did for example in my essay on Theognis. . . . It would be miserable not to be able to write better and yet want to so badly. . . .

In short, dear friend, one can't go one's way independently enough. Truth seldom resides where temples are built and priests ordained for her. What we do wisely or foolishly we ourselves have to sweat out, not those who give us good or bad counsel. We ought at least to be allowed the pleasure of committing follies freely. A universal recipe for helping each individual simply doesn't exist. One must be one's own physician, indeed one's own laboratory. We consider our own well-being too little, our egotism isn't intelligent enough, our intellect isn't egotistic enough. . . .

6   TO CARL VON GERSDORFF

Naumburg [24 November and] 1 December 1867[1]
. . . I spent the last days of my Böhmerwald trip in Meiningen. For there a grand four-day music festival had been organized by the futurists, who had chosen this place to celebrate their strange musical orgies. The Abbé Liszt presided. This school has now dedicated itself to Schopenhauer with fervor. A symphonic poem by Hans von Bülow, "Nir-

Nietzsche's parents, Ludwig and Franziska Nietzsche

Nietzsche as a young man   Elisabeth Förster-Nietzsche

vana," had for its libretto an arrangement of Schopen-hauerian theses, but the music was frightful. Liszt himself, on the other hand, captured the spirit of that Indian Nirvana splendidly in several of his liturgical compositions. . . .

. . . Later I took part in the philologists' convention in Halle — and fate struck.

For I am now an artillery man in the second mounted detachment of field artillery regiment No. 4.

. . . Only now am I really grateful to our Schopenhauer, now that I have occasion to practice a little self-denial. During the first five weeks I even had to do stable duty: at 5:30 each morning I was in the stable to clean out the manure and to groom the horse with comb and brush. . . . The riding lessons give me the most pleasure. I have a very handsome horse and am said to have a knack for riding. When I'm galloping about the large parade ground on my Balduin, I'm very content with my lot. . . .

[1] The source for this letter is *HKG Br* II, 164–166.

7   TO PAUL DEUSSEN
[Leipzig, late October 1868]
. . . You don't write a critique of a world-view at all; either you understand it or you don't. No other attitude makes sense to me. Someone who doesn't smell the fragrance of a rose must not be allowed to criticize it. But if he does smell it, what joy![1] He loses all desire to criticize. . . .

[1] Nietzsche uses the expression *à la bonheur,* which is grammatically impossible, since *bonheur* is masculine. He is presumably thinking confusedly of the familiar *à la bonne heure*! ("wonderful!").

8   TO ERWIN ROHDE
[Leipzig, 22 and 28 February 1869]
My dear friend, today, on Schopenhauer's birthday, I have no one with whom I could talk as intimately as with you. I live here in an ashen cloud of loneliness, the more so

as on all sides convivial arms are linked with mine and I give in almost nightly to the dreary press of invitations. In these gatherings I hear so many voices that I cannot find my own. How on earth is it possible to put up with this buzzing din? . . .

This philistinism is getting on my nerves, — but none of my local acquaintances notices a thing. They let themselves be dazzled by the title "Professor"[1] and believe that I'm the happiest man under the sun. . . .

[1] Nietzsche had just heard of his Basel appointment.

9 TO RICHARD WAGNER
[Basel, 22 May 1869]
Very honored Sir, how long I've wanted to express, for once without any reserve, the measure of my gratitude to you. Truly the best and loftiest moments of my life are linked with your name, and there is only one other man, your great soulmate Arthur Schopenhauer, whom I equally revere, indeed almost worship. . . .

. . . If I have thus far held fast to our Germanic seriousness of purpose, to a deepened sense of this enigmatic and hazardous state of being, I owe it to you and Schopenhauer. . . .

Your most faithful and devoted disciple and admirer,
Dr. Nietzsche, Prof. in Basel

10 TO ERWIN ROHDE
[Basel, late January and mid-February 1870]
. . . I miss you unbelievably, so bring me the comfort of your presence and see to it that it's not for too short a time. It is an entirely new experience for me to have absolutely *no one* around to whom I can tell what's best and most burdensome in my life. And not even a really sympathetic colleague. Under such hermitlike circumstances, at so tender and troubled an age, my friendship is becoming

pathological. I beg you as an invalid begs — "come to Basel!". . .

By the way, you'd be wise not to choose such a small university as a place to settle down. You become isolated even in your discipline. What I wouldn't give if we could live together! I'm actually forgetting how to talk. But the most depressing thing is that I have to keep playing a teacher, a philologist, a somebody, and that I immediately have to prove myself to everyone I deal with. I'm really very bad at that, and more and more I keep forgetting how it's done. I become tongue-tied, or I deliberately say only as much as a well-bred man of the world might be given to say. In short, I'm more dissatisfied with myself than with the world, and for that reason all the more committed to what really matters most.

Mid-February. . . . I gave a lecture here on "Socrates and Tragedy,"[1] which aroused shock and misunderstanding. But it brought me even closer to my friends in Tribschen. There may be hope yet: even Richard Wagner has given me to understand in the most moving way what sort of destiny he sees marked out for me. All this is very scary. And you know what Ritschl had to say about me. Still, I refuse to let myself be troubled. I have no literary ambition whatever, and as I don't aspire to glittering and lofty places, I don't need to tie myself to a prevailing norm. On the contrary I'd like, when it is time, to say my piece as seriously and openly as possible. Scholarship, art, and philosophy are growing together inside me to such an extent that one day I'm bound to give birth to centaurs. . . .

[1] This lecture presented in an earlier and much briefer version some of the central concepts of *The Birth of Tragedy.*

11 TO RICHARD WAGNER

Basel, 21 May 1870

Pater Seraphice . . .

Allow me to express my birthday wishes today in as narrowly personal a way as possible. Others may congratulate you in the name of holy art, in the name of the finest German aspirations, in the name of your own deepest desires. But for me the most subjective of wishes will suffice: May you continue to do what you've done for me in the past year—initiate me into the mysteries of art and life. Even if, seen through philology's gray mists, I sometimes seem remote from you, I never really am, my thoughts hover around you constantly. If what you once wrote—how proud I was—is true, namely that music rules my spirit, it is you who are the conductor of my music. And you yourself told me that even something mediocre, directed well, can make a pleasing impression. . . .

One of the "Blissful Youths"[1]

[1] Pater Seraphicus and the Blissful Youths figure in Goethe's *Faust*, Part Two.

12 TO ERWIN ROHDE

[Basel, 19 July 1870]

. . . A terrifying thunderclap here: the Franco-Prussian war has been declared, and our whole sleazy culture is falling headlong into the arms of the most appalling demon. The things we're about to witness! Friend, dearest friend, we saw each other for the last time in the twilight of peace. How grateful I am to you! If your existence becomes unbearable for you now, come back to me. What do all our aspirations matter now!

We may already be at the beginning of the end. What a wasteland! Once again we shall need monasteries. And we shall be the first *fratres*.

The true Swiss

13 TO RICHARD WAGNER

Erlangen [11 September 1870]

Dear and revered Master . . .

. . . My work as an orderly is ended for the time being,

alas because of illness. My many duties took me near Metz, where my very reliable friend Mosengel and I were able to finish the bulk of our business successfully. In Ars sur Moselle we took over some of the wounded and then returned with them to Germany. This three day and three night intimacy with severely wounded men was the hardest thing we had to do. Throughout this time I had to nurse six of the poor wretches by myself in a miserable cattle car. All had bones shot through, some had been wounded in four places; on top of that I found two cases of gangrene. That I could endure this pest-infested stench, that I was even able to eat and sleep, seems miraculous to me now.

But I had hardly delivered my cargo to a military hospital in Karlsruhe when unmistakable symptoms of disease appeared in me as well. With effort I made it to Erlangen to report to my group. Then I took to bed, and have stayed there. A very capable doctor diagnosed first severe dysentery and then laryngeal diphtheria as well. But we advanced on both of these contagious devils with the greatest possible vigor, and today the prospects seem hopeful. I've made my acquaintance with these two well-known scourges of the infirmary, then, at the same time; they've made such short work of exhausting me that for now I must give up any further thought of volunteer service and think only of my own recovery. And so, after a mere four weeks of trying to do a bit for the common weal, I'm already thrown back on myself again—a miserable state of affairs! . . .

14 TO CARL VON GERSDORFF

Basel, 7 November 1870

. . . Last night I had a treat I would have shared with you above all others. Jacob Burckhardt gave a public lecture on "Historical Greatness"[1]—entirely within the scope of our own thoughts and feelings. This elderly, most singular man is disposed to conceal, though not falsify, the truth; but during intimate walks he calls Schopenhauer "our philosopher." I'm attending a one-hour-a-week lecture course of his on the study of history, and I think I am the only one in the class of sixty who follows his deep trains of thought, with their strange breaks and twists whenever they touch on something delicate. For the first time I am really enjoying a lecture course; but then it's the sort that I myself could give if I were older. In his lecture today he took up Hegel's philosophy of history, in a way altogether worthy of the Centennial. . . .[2]

I'm deeply apprehensive about our impending cultural situation. If only we aren't made to pay too dearly for our colossal material successes, in a domain in which *I* at least would not consent to any kind of setback. Between ourselves: I regard present-day Prussia as a power highly dangerous for civilization. . . .

[1] Cf. chapter five of *World-Historical Reflections,* published posthumously.

[2] Hegel was born on 27 August 1770.

15 TO CARL VON GERSDORFF
Basel, 12 December 1870

My dear friend, how happy I'll be if you are not among the past weeks' many casualties and have survived unscathed! One doesn't dare think about these horrible things, lest one lose all courage.

But I am determined to write to you now, hoping, indeed taking for granted, that you have escaped even these awful perils, brave and fortunate, the beloved of the God of War — but without loving him back! . . .

. . . Give me a few years more and you should sense a new influence on classical studies, and hopefully bound up with it a new spirit at work in the scientific and moral upbringing of our nation.

But what devils are spawning in the bloody soil of this war to undermine our faith! I'm prepared for the worst, even while trusting that, amid this surfeit of horror and suffering, here and there the flower of insight will bloom in the night. Our struggle is still ahead of us — *that's why we must live!* That's also why I have faith that you are leading a charmed life; the shells meant to do us in will not be shot from rifles or cannons. . . .

16 TO ERWIN ROHDE

[Basel, 15 December 1870]

. . . At long last I too understand what Schopenhauer's reflections on academic wisdom are all about. A really radical living for truth just isn't possible in a university. Nothing revolutionary will ever come out of such a place.

And we can become true teachers only when we lift ourselves out of this atmosphere by every available means, when we become not just wiser but *better* men. Here I feel more than anything else the need to be genuine — another reason why I won't be able to put up with the air of the academy much longer.

So we will throw off this yoke once and for all: for me that's settled. And then we'll build a new *Greek* academy. . . . I am preparing a clarion-call to everyone who hasn't already choked to death or been swallowed up by the contemporary scene. . . . My plan may strike you as an erratic whim. It *isn't*; it is a *necessity*.

Wagner's new book, on Beethoven, can tell you a lot about what I now want from the future. Read it. It is a revelation of the spirit in which *we* shall one day live.

Even if we find few soulmates, I still think that — admittedly at some cost — we can tear ourselves out of this maelstrom and reach a small island on which we'd no longer have to plug our ears with wax. Then we would be each other's teachers, our books would serve merely as bait to recruit people for our monastic-artistic fellowship.[1] We would live, play, and work for one another — perhaps that's the only way one can work "for all mankind."

To show you how serious I am, I've already begun to

limit my everyday needs in order to lay aside a small amount of my income. We should try our luck in the lotteries too. And when we write books, I shall demand from now on the highest possible honoraria. . . .

[1] The closest Nietzsche ever came to realizing this recurrent dream was the winter in Sorrento, 1876–1877, spent in the company of Malwida von Meysenbug, Paul Rée, and the young student Albert Brenner.

17 TO WILHELM VISCHER[1]

[Basel, presumably January 1871]

Most honored Councillor, for the following plan I have an unusually great need of your good advice and oft-tested genuine concern for me. You will see that I have kept the welfare of the University sharply in view, and that it is her true interest that has forced me to the following rather detailed account.

My doctors will have informed you to what degree I am once again ailing, and that overexertion is to blame for this unbearable condition. Now I have asked myself repeatedly what accounts for its onset in the middle of almost every semester; I have even had to consider giving up for good my work at the University, as a way of life for which I am constitutionally unfit. But at last I've arrived at a different view of the matter, which I want to lay before you now.

I am living here in a peculiar state of conflict, and it is this that is exhausting and even destroying me physically. Compelled by nature to think some one thing through philosophically and to stick with a problem steadfastly and uninterruptedly in long trains of thought, I keep finding myself tossed about and derailed by the manifold daily demands of my profession. I won't be able to stand this jumble of Pedagogical Institute and University much longer, since I feel that my real, *philosophical* task, to which if need be I shall sacrifice any career, is suffering, even to the point of being reduced to a mere sideline. . . .

In this frame of mind, I am taking the liberty of asking

you to consider me a candidate for the philosophy professorship vacated by Teichmüller.

Concerning my personal qualifications for the philosophy chair, I must put my own testimony first: I believe myself to possess the needed capacity and learning and, everything considered, I think I am more qualified for this position than for a purely philological one. Those who know me from my student days have never doubted the predominance of my philosophical bent; and even in my philological studies I was chiefly attracted by what seemed to me important either for the history of philosophy or for ethical and esthetic problems. . . . Indeed one of my deepest desires would be fulfilled if in this respect too I could follow the voice of my nature. And I have reason to suspect that after settling the above-mentioned conflict my physical condition would greatly improve as well. . . . Of the more recent philosophers I have studied Kant and Schopenhauer with particular interest. Over the past two years you have surely learned to trust in my ability to avoid what is improper and offensive, and to distinguish what is appropriate from what isn't in lectures to students.

If I may lay my entire scheme before you now: I think that you would find in Rohde an exceptionally suitable successor for my philological chair and my position in the Pedagogical Institute. Of all the younger philologists I have come across, R., whom I have known extremely well for four years, is the ablest — a true gem for any university that gets him. What's more, he can still be got, although I hear that Kiel is thinking about tying him up permanently through the creation of a new special professorship in philology. I cannot adequately express how much my existence here in Basel would be made easier by the presence of my best friend. . . .

[1] Wilhelm Vischer, a well-known classicist and professor of philology at the University of Basel, had used his influence as president of the University's board of trustees, president of the Pedagogical Institute (in which Nietzsche was required to teach part-time) and member of the city council to facilitate Nietzsche's exceptional appointment two years earlier.

Lugano [29 March 1871]

Yes, my dear friend, to break the spell! That's not easy, and for me just now quite impossible. For I know nothing, absolutely nothing about how our business is progressing. Vischer did indeed write me here once, but in his letter there was no mention of our common concern. And back in Basel, before I left but after I wrote you, several things led me to believe that the "philosopher" Steffensen is not well disposed toward the project. Just think how vulnerable I am if they can bring up my never very clandestine Schopenhauerizing! So I'd best establish my philosophical credentials a bit. For that purpose a small piece, *Origin and End of Tragedy*,[1] has been completed except for a few brushstrokes. . . .

Alas, my physical condition still leaves much to be desired. Every other night is a sleepless one. . . .

. . . I live in reckless estrangement from philology — a deeper alienation is hardly imaginable. Praise and censure, indeed the highest tributes from this quarter make my flesh creep. So bit by bit I'm claiming my philosophical estate, and already believe in myself; it wouldn't even surprise me if I blossomed into a poet. I just don't seem to have a compass to tell me what I'm destined for. And yet in looking back everything seems to fit so well that it's as if a guiding spirit has been showing me the way. I never thought that anyone so confused about his aims, and devoid of that higher striving which covets state posts, could still feel as clearheaded and serene as I on the whole do. What an experience, to see your own world, like a pretty ball, grow round and full before your eyes — here some new metaphysics, there a new esthetic, then a new principle of education utterly repudiating our high schools and universities. I no longer learn anything which doesn't at once fit perfectly into some nook of what's already in hand. . . . Pride and mania are words really too weak to describe my spiritual sleeplessness. And so I can now see my whole university career as something secondary, often simply painful. Even the philosophy professorship is something I want mainly for your sake, since I see it too as a mere stopgap.

Oh how I long for good health! You have to have a project expected to outlast your own lifetime to be really grateful for every good night's sleep, for every warm ray of sunshine, yes even for "regularity." As it is, some of my lower internal organs seem to be ruined. Hence bad nerves, insomnia, hemorrhoids, coughing up blood, etc. But do be kind enough not to trace the aforementioned state of mind to my ganglial condition, or I'll fear for my immortality. Besides, I've never known flatulence to provide the ideal atmosphere for philosophizing. . . .

[1] This was an earlier title for what was shortly to become *The Birth of Tragedy.*

19   TO RICHARD WAGNER

Basel, 2 January 1872

Most revered Master, at long last my New Year's greeting, and a Christmas offering. . . .[1]

May my essay justify at least in some measure the active interest you've always taken, to my great embarrassment, in its growth. . . . On every page you'll find me but trying to thank you for all you've given me, and the only doubt that plagues me is whether I've always properly received it. Perhaps later I'll be able to do a lot of it better — and by later I mean the period of fulfillment, the period of Bayreuth Culture. Meanwhile I feel proud that I've been baptized, and that from now on whenever I am mentioned it will be in connection with you. God have mercy on my philologists if they refuse to learn anything now. . . .

[1] *The Birth of Tragedy out of the Spirit of Music,* published in Leipzig, December 1871, with a dedicatory preface to Wagner.

20 TO ERWIN ROHDE

Basel, 28 January 1872

My good and dear friend, I've just been approached through Susemihl as to whether I'd accept a professorship in Greifswald, but at once said no, recommending you instead. . . . Word got out, and the good citizens of Basel rallied round me. Although I protested that it was a mere feeler and no firm offer, the students, wishing to express how much they admire what I've been doing here, resolved on a torchlight parade. But I wouldn't allow one.[1]

I'm currently giving lectures on "The Future of Our Educational Institutions"; they're causing something of a sensation. . . .

I've formed an alliance with Wagner. You can't imagine how close we are now and how our plans mesh.

The things I've heard about my book are beyond belief—which is why I'm not writing anything about them. — What do you think? I am profoundly sobered by all I hear of it, since I divine in such voices the fate in store for what is still to come. This life will yet be hard. . . .

[1] The University of Basel responded by raising Nietzsche's salary. Bernoulli (I, 437) mentions an offer to Nietzsche to become *Gymnasialdirektor* (headmaster) in Heidelberg around this time, suggesting that Nietzsche's reputation as an educator was growing rapidly.

21 TO FRIEDRICH RITSCHL

Basel, 30 January 1872

Most honored Councillor, I trust you won't take amiss my astonishment at not having heard a single word from you about my recently published book — or for that matter my candor in telling you of this astonishment. The book, after all, is a kind of manifesto, and least of all invites silence. Perhaps you'll be amazed at the reaction I took for granted on your part, my revered teacher. I thought that if you had ever encountered anything encouraging in your life, it might be this book, full of hope for our study of antiquity, full of hope for the German spirit. . . . And though I seek no personal advantage, I do intend to accomplish something for others. I'm above all concerned with capturing the younger generation of philologists, and I would consider it a disgrace if I were to fail in this regard. —I must say your silence is somewhat disturbing.[1]. . .

[1] Ritschl's comment in his diary concerning *The Birth of Tragedy* on New Year's Eve, 1871 (the advance copy had just come from Leipzig) was: "inspired dissoluteness." Curt Wachsmuth, editor of the Ritschl-Nietzsche correspondence, comments: "One could hardly expect that a scholar so far removed from Dionysian ecstatic mysticism as Ritschl would receive the book with exultation. He was disappointed, shook his head—and remained silent." (*G Br* III, 138.) Ritschl finally did reply to Nietzsche's unequivocal demand for a response on 14 February 1872. He begged off a thoroughgoing critique on the grounds of age (65), long conditioning in almost antithetical directions, and unfamiliarity with the Schopenhauerian philosophical seedbed of Nietzsche's new perspectives. He hoped his young friend would understand an old pedagogue's misgivings concerning the value of the book as a basis for educational reform. Might Nietzsche's path not "lead the majority of our youth to an immature disdain for scholarship, without replacing it by a heightened sensitivity to art"? Might it not "open the floodgates to universal dilettantism"? (*Ibid.,* pp. 141–142.) Nietzsche took this response rather well, encouraged by the friendly terms in which it was couched. Cordial personal and professional relations were maintained for some time thereafter.

22 TO CARL VON GERSDORFF

Basel, 4 February 1872

. . . Whatever you do, bear in mind that we two have been called to fight and work in the vanguard of a cultural movement which might take a generation, perhaps longer, to filter down to the broader mass. May this be our pride, may this inspire us. It is my belief that we were not born to be happy, but to do our duty; and we should consider ourselves blessed to know where our duty lies.

It's becoming very hard for my book to get a hearing. An excellent review which Rohde did for the *Literarisches Zentralblatt* was rejected by the editorial staff. There went the *last* chance that a serious voice in a learned journal would speak out in support of it. From now on I expect nothing but malice and stupidity. But I'm counting on a slow, quiet journey—centuries long, I'm convinced. For some eternal truths are spoken here for the first time. They're bound to reverberate. I'm unconcerned about myself; I want nothing for myself, least of all a career. . . .

23 TO CARL VON GERSDORFF

Basel, 1 May 1872

. . . Rohde too will be going to Bayreuth.[1] He telegraphed from Kiel yesterday to say he'd been made professor there. Could you perhaps send him a few lines of congratulations? He has something fine up his sleeve about Wagner and me, but I mustn't give it away yet. The first review of my book has appeared—guess where? In the Italian *Rivista Europea*! Did I tell you about von Bülow's enthusiasm? And that he is going to dedicate a book to me? And that he said there'd soon be need for a second edition of mine? . . .

Last Saturday was a sad and deeply moving farewell to Tribschen. Tribschen is all over now. We wandered about as though among ruins. Nostalgia lay everywhere, in the air, in the clouds. The dog wouldn't eat, the servants couldn't stop sobbing whenever someone spoke to them. Together we packed the manuscripts, the letters, the books —oh it was so sad! These three years I spent near Tribschen, during which I paid twenty-three visits there—what they mean to me! What would I be without them? . . .

[1] Gersdorff, together with several friends in Berlin, had been propagating the Wagnerian cause and helping raise funds for the opening of Bayreuth. The foundation stone for the *Festspielhaus* was laid on 22 May, with the Master himself conducting Beethoven's Ninth Symphony.

24 TO CARL VON GERSDORFF

[Basel, 10 June 1872]

My dear friend, so that you won't be the least bit worried about me and won't imagine me upset in any way, I am writing to tell you that I read the pamphlet and was at once completely reassured. Not a word strikes home! Everything, down to the smallest detail, is distortion, misunderstanding, and malice. The little fellow really deserves a spanking; a letter from Rohde should presently make clear to you what form it is to take.

I feel heartfelt sorrow for this deluded young man,[1] and like you feel genuine regret when I think of his good name. But it can't be helped. He must be punished publicly. Among ourselves, though, we should not forget that such is the fruit of the education and philology of our time. Should Wilamowitz carry a scar to the end of his days, let it be his constant reminder of how shamefully he has been misled, seduced, and egged on, and how badly he was educated.

I think, my dear friend, that I now have one more experience under my belt, a typical one; and that I also know something now that I didn't know before: how I can take this sort of thing. I face the future bolder and better armed than ever, and the outlines of a new essay (*not yet* the pedagogical one) are growing inside me. Calm, contemplativeness, and just plain contentment set in again, as soon as I'd read the piece.

So don't be depressed, and think of our Bayreuth community. We friends now have everything in common!

---

[1] Ulrich von Wilamowitz-Möllendorff, then twenty-four, had in May written a polemic of about thirty pages entitled *Philology of the Future! A Reply to F. N.'s Birth of Tragedy*. It was an impassioned defense of the tradition of classical scholarship (a domain in which Wilamowitz was later to excel) against the author's "fancied originality and insolent array of assertions, standing in direct proportion to his ignorance and lack of love for truth." Part of Nietzsche's thinly disguised anger stems from the fact that in the fall of the previous year Wilamowitz had come to Naumburg to pay him what he regarded as a friendly, even deferential visit.

25 TO GUSTAV KRUG[1]

Basel, 24 July 1872

... I've fallen in love with your music; I only wish I were more of a musician, so that I could drink it in with even less effort. ... Really, my dear friend, nothing more need come of you, for you have already become something: a first-class musician—while I make an ass of myself with "Dionysian" and "Apollonian." How splendid it always is to really do something, rather than just theorizing! ... I for my part have sworn off music-making again for the next six years. ... Don't let your musical sensibility be contaminated, especially by the barbarous air which my own music breathes. I'm quite without illusions—right now, at least.

[1] Gustav Krug (1844–1902) was a friend of Nietzsche's from their childhood days in Naumburg. He published several volumes of hymns and songs, and set a number of Nietzsche's poems to music. It was Krug who first introduced Nietzsche to Wagner's music in 1861.

26 TO ERWIN ROHDE

Basel, 25 October 1872

... I don't know how to put in words what you've done for me.[1] I would have been so completely incapable of doing it for myself, and I know that there is no one else from whom I could have hoped for such a gift. What self-control it must have taken, my poor dear friend, to have to deal with that fellow at such length! ... Leipzig speaks with one voice about my book: ... it is the sheerest nonsense, with which absolutely nothing can be done; whoever wrote that book is dead to the learned world. It is as if I'd committed a crime. ...

Should we be very disturbed that there are so few spectators who have eyes to see the race we are running? Should we care, when we know that these few spectators are also the only competent judges? I for one am ready to relinquish to a spectator like Wagner every laurel wreath the present age has to give. The desire to satisfy him drives me harder than any other force. It's so difficult, you see—he minces no words, says exactly what he likes and dislikes, and acts as my conscience, punishing and rewarding. . . .

[1] Rohde had just written a forty-six-page rebuttal of Wilamowitz's *Philology of the Future!* entitled *Pseudophilology* and presented in the form of "a philologist's open letter to Richard Wagner," who had himself written an open letter to Nietzsche in June. Rohde's polemic opens with a jaunty aphorism from Lichtenberg: "When a head and a book bump together, and there's a hollow ring, is it always the book that's to blame?" But before getting down to the business of erudite refutation, Rohde stops to place the squabble in a larger perspective. Wilamowitz obviously is not speaking for himself alone. "To the great majority of present-day philologists it will seem utterly paradoxical that a writer should even make a serious effort to employ philological scholarship for something more than the sheer exercise of intellectual acumen and a good memory, let alone appeal beyond these precious and indispensable capacities to higher powers of perception, so as finally—in the words of Gorgias—to woo not the waiting women, but the noble Penelope herself, i.e. the highest prize of classical studies, an understanding of the noblest works of art, which in turn could once again lead us to a fruitful living art."

The size of the guns trained on him, Wilamowitz concluded in a rejoinder to Rohde that appeared early in 1873, must indicate that his critique had struck home. Wagner in any case seems to agree with him on one point, namely that Nietzsche should get out of philology! But admittedly something far worse than lack of scholarly acuity on Nietzsche's part had tried Wilamowitz's patience. "I saw here the evolution of millennia repudiated; here the timeless disclosures of philosophy and religion were effaced so that in the desert left behind a confused pessimism could cut its sweet and sour capers; here the divine images with which poetry and the plastic arts had peopled our sky were smashed to bits in order to worship the idol Richard Wagner in their dust. . . ."

 27 TO MALWIDA VON MEYSENBUG

Basel, 7 November 1872

. . . For the whole third week in November a splendid visit is in store for me, right here in Basel! The visit-in-itself—Wagner and wife.[1] They are on a grand tour of all

Erwin Rohde, Carl von Gersdorff,
and Nietzsche

Franz Overbeck

Hans von Bülow

Carl von Gersdorff

the major German theaters, and will take this opportunity to visit our famous Basel *dentist,* to whom therefore I am most deeply indebted. Wagner's latest treatise, "On Actors and Singers"—have you seen it? But you surely haven't yet seen the *apologia* written with sword and pen by Prof. Rohde of Kiel, far superior to anything his enemies can muster. My *Birth of Tragedy,* you see, has made me the most obnoxious philologist around, defending whom is virtually a miracle of daring, since the order of the day is to condemn me. Aside from the polemic, with which I don't want to burden you, Rohde's essay says a number of good things about the philological foundations of my book; these should be of some interest to you. If only I didn't have to fear that this generous move on Rohde's part will throw him into a snakepit of ill-will and spite. Now the two of us are on the Index together! . . .

Most esteemed lady, what you have undergone was indeed worse, though similar, and who knows how much my life may yet come to resemble yours. For until now I've barely begun to express myself; I shall need a stout heart and strength-giving friendship, above all inspiring examples, if I'm not to run out of breath in midstream. Yes, good examples! So I think of you and feel joy in my heart, esteemed Fräulein, at having come to know you, a solitary fighter for what is right. Believe once and for all that I have placed in you the unqualified trust which in this mistrustful world only my closest friends inspire—and that I felt that way about you from the moment we met. Fräulein Olga[2] too should rest assured that she can count on me come what may. I'm truly very fond of you both, and hope for opportunities to prove it.

But now here is your friendly letter from Florence to pull me up short, making me realize that my deplorable silence must have created a very different impression from the one suggested just now in this letter I'd set aside and left unfinished. Why didn't I write for so long a time? Astonished, I ask myself the same question, without being able to find proper reasons or even excuses. This is something I have experienced before — finding it hardest to write to those who are most often in my thoughts. But I don't understand it. Do interpret this as charitably as possible and then let it be forgotten. There is so much that is irrational, for which the only remedy is just to forget it.

With this dark saying I want to end today. Enclosed: the photo, Rohde's essay, and my five lectures about the future of our educational institutions. Bear in mind as you read these a very specific Basel audience. It would now strike me as impossible to allow something like this to be printed, for it doesn't go deep enough, and is built around a device[3] whose inventiveness is meager indeed. . . .

[1] This visit didn't materialize. There was a meeting in Strasbourg instead.

[2] Olga Herzen, Malwida von Meysenbug's adopted daughter.

[3] Two student friends, celebrating the end of the summer semester in a forest overlooking the Rhine, interrupt their conventional revelries to eavesdrop on an animated discussion about education between a cranky old philosopher (Schopenhauer) and his pupil. Eventually they become so fascinated that they join in.

28 TO RICHARD WAGNER

[Basel, mid-November 1872]

Beloved Master, in view of all that has happened lately I have no right whatever to be discontent, for I bask in the warm sun of fraternal love, comfort, and reviving hopes. Yet one thing disturbs me very greatly at present: our winter semester has begun and I have no students! Our philologists have failed to appear! . . . The fact is easy to explain: I have suddenly fallen into such disrepute in my profession that our little university is being made to suffer for it. This torments me, for I am really very devoted and grateful to it, and want least of all to do it harm. . . . Until last semester the enrollment in philology had steadily risen — and now it is as though it had blown away! . . .

29 TO RICHARD WAGNER

Basel, 18 April 1873

Most revered Master, I live in constant recollection of the Bayreuth days, and I see the many things I learned and experienced there in so very short a time spread out before me in ever greater fullness. If you were dissatisfied with me when I visited you last, I understand only too well, without being able to do anything about it. I learn and perceive things very slowly, yet every moment I am with you I meet something I've never thought of before and yearn to make mine. I fully realize, dearest Master, that such company can give you no pleasure; indeed it must be unbearable at times. How often I have longed for at least the semblance of a greater freedom and independence, but in vain. Enough. I beg you, accept me as but a pupil, pen in hand and notebook poised—a pupil whose talent, for that matter, is very sluggish and by no means versatile. Day by day I become more melancholy, wanting so much to help somehow, to be of use to you; but I seem utterly incapable of it, and don't even contribute anything to your diversion and amusement.

Or perhaps I may yet, once I've finished what's currently in hand, an attack on the famous author David Strauss.[1]. . .

[1] Wagner was more than diverted by the essay, which became the first of the *Untimely Reflections*. Nietzsche, writing to Gersdorff on 27 September 1873, quotes Wagner as having told him: "I've been reading in it again, and I swear to God that I consider you to be the only one who knows what I want!" (*HKG Br* IV, 11.)

30 TO CARL VON GERSDORFF

Basel, 1 April 1874

Dear trusted friend, if only you didn't have much too high an opinion of me! I fear you may be in for a disappointment; let me give you a first taste of it. I know myself, and assure you that I have done nothing to merit your praise. If only you realized what melancholy and despair I feel,

deep down, when I look at myself as a productive being! . . .
There can be no talk of genuine achievement as long as one
remains so burdened and shackled. Will I ever be free?
Doubt begets doubt. The goal is too distant, and even if you
do get pretty close to it, the long struggle has most likely
consumed your energies. By the time freedom is in sight
you're as spent as a salmon approaching the spawning-
ground. That really frightens me. It's awful to be so conscious, so soon, of your destiny. . . . Just now I've had it up
to here.

My health, by the way, is excellent: rest assured. But
I'm quite unhappy with Nature for not having given me a
little more understanding, and a fuller heart. The best
things keep eluding me. To know this is the greatest an-
guish a man can feel. . . .

My writings are said to be so dark and incomprehensible!
I thought that if one spoke of dire straits, those in them
would understand. Surely that's so. But where are those in
dire straits? . . .

31 TO MALWIDA VON MEYSENBUG
Basel, 25 October 1874
. . . There is nothing I want more than to gain insight
into that whole extremely complicated system of antago-
nisms of which the "modern world" consists. Fortunately,
I'm lacking in all political and social ambition, so that I
have nothing to fear from that quarter — no distractions, no
need for compromise or concern. In short, I can say what I
think, and I intend to find out to what degree our friends,
who are so proud of their freedom of thought, can actually
tolerate free thoughts. . . . Now, confidentially, I'd like to
find myself a good wife quite soon, and then I can look on
my life's desires as fulfilled. . . .

32 TO CARL VON GERSDORFF

[Basel, June 1875]

Dear friend, my sister was very grateful for your letter and your sincere concern; but I want to tell you myself how I am. I've been through a *very bad* time, and there may be an even worse one to come. My stomach could no longer be tamed, even with an absurdly strict diet. Chronic headaches of the fiercest sort, which lasted for days. Vomiting on an empty stomach, for hours on end. In short the machine seemed to want to disintegrate, and I won't deny having wished several times that it would do just that. Great fatigue, difficulty getting about, hypersensitivity to light. . . . Under these conditions it became necessary, with my good sister's help, to improve my domestic arrangements. We have a place, near the old one, and will move in after summer vacation. . . . We will see what can be done to perfect a daily routine. . . .

33 TO CARL VON GERSDORFF

[Basel, 13 December 1875]

Yesterday, my beloved friend, your letter came, and this morning, right at the start of a week of hard work, your books. . . . Really, I marvel at the fine instinct in your friendship (I hope the expression doesn't strike you as too animal-like), at your hitting upon these Indian maxims just when for the past two months I've been looking toward India with a growing thirst. . . . The conviction that life is worthless and that all goals are delusions comes over me so strongly, above all when I'm lying sick in bed, that I long to hear more about that country, hopefully something free of Judaeo-Christian phraseology. . . .

I'm working at ridding myself of the *urgency* in the will-to-know; all scholars suffer from it, and it is this that deprives them of the wonderful calm that should come in the wake of insights achieved. For the present I'm still stretched so tautly between the various demands of my occupation that I have been made to feel this urgency all too often.

Gradually I'll put things right. Then I'll have better health too, something I won't achieve until I've earned it, until . . . only that one drive, the will-to-know, remains and I've been freed of all other drives and desires. A simple household, a well regulated day, no unsettling ambitions or cravings for companionship, life with my sister (thanks to which everything around me becomes wholly Nietzschean and remarkably peaceful), the knowledge that I have excellent and loving friends, the possession of forty good books from sundry peoples and times (and even more not exactly bad ones), the lasting good fortune to have found Schopenhauer and Wagner as educators and the Greeks for my daily work, the conviction that I won't be lacking good students from now on — that's my current life. Alas I cannot omit the chronic torment which every fortnight lays hold of me for nearly two whole days, sometimes longer. Oh well, this can't last forever.

My old and true friend, we've already been through quite a bit together: youth, experience, education, liking and loathing, aspiration and hope. . . . You have a splendid capacity for sharing joy; I find this to be still rarer and nobler than the ability to feel compassion.

34 TO CARL VON GERSDORFF
[Basel, 18 January 1876][1]
. . . It's an effort to write, so I'll be brief. Dearest friend, I've just been through the worst, the most painful, the most dismal Christmas I've ever known. On the very first day, after numerous danger signals, there was a real breakdown. I could no longer doubt that I was in the throes of a serious disease of the brain, and that only this center could cause so much pain in my stomach and eyes. My father died at thirty-six of brain-fever; it's possible that I'll go even sooner. Now . . . after a week of total debility and excruciating pain, I'm a little better again, though by no means convalescent: every moment there's a reminder that the rotten state of affairs has not gone away. I've been relieved

at the Pedagogical Institute till Easter, and am back teaching at the University.[2] I'm patient, but full of misgivings about what's ahead. I'm living almost entirely on milk, which is good for me, and sleeping well. Milk and sleep are the best things I have now. If only the frightful attacks, which last all day, would cease! Without these I could at least drag myself from one day to the next.

My sister reads to me a lot, since reading and writing are hard on me. I should have mentioned Walter Scott along with milk and sleep. . . . My mother will arrive here shortly.

Please keep the contents of this letter to yourself. We don't want the Bayreuthers upset. . . .

May you, at least, fare well. More and more I have to seek my happiness in the good fortune of my friends. All my own plans are like wisps of smoke: I see them ahead of me and want to clutch them. For it is wretched to live without them, indeed hardly possible. . . .

Soon there'll be better news from Basel, I promise you.

[1] The source for this letter is *HKG Br* IV, 251–253.

[2] But on 22 February Nietzsche reports to Gersdorff that he has had to suspend all lecturing (*ibid.*, p. 255).

 TO MATHILDE TRAMPEDACH[1]

Geneva, 11 April 1876

My dear Fräulein! Since you're writing something for me this evening, I want to write something for you as well. —

Gather all the strength that is in your heart so that you will not be frightened by the question I now put to you: Will you be my wife? I love you, and I feel as though you were already mine. Not a word about how quickly I've fallen! At least there's nothing improper about it, so there's no need to apologize for anything. What I want to know is whether you feel as I do — that we were never strangers, not even for a moment! Don't you share my faith that together each of us could become freer and better than we could separately, and so "excelsior"? . . .

Do be candid and keep nothing back. No one but our mutual friend Herr von Senger knows about this letter and what it contains. I'm taking the 11 o'clock express to Basel tomorrow—I have to get back. My Basel address is enclosed. If you can say yes to my question, I shall write at once to your mother (whose address I'd need). If you can bring yourself to make a quick decision, a note arriving by 10 o'clock tomorrow would reach me in time.

Wishing you all that is blessed and good for ever more,

Friedrich Nietzsche

[1] Nietzsche had just met Frl. Trampedach here through Hugo von Senger, music teacher, virtuoso, and conductor. A twenty-one-year-old Russo-German of exceptional beauty and grace, she is alleged to have resembled Fra Filippo Lippi's women. (Brann, p. 42.) Nietzsche was enchanted with her, and so taken with her recitation of Longfellow's "Excelsior" (in German) that he asked her to write out a copy for him. It would seem that he misinterpreted her friendliness and natural warmth. At this time she was already closely tied to von Senger, whose second wife she later became. Her reply to Nietzsche's proposal no longer exists.

36 TO MALWIDA VON MEYSENBUG

Basel, Good Friday, 14 April 1876

Highly esteemed lady, about two weeks ago I spent a Sunday at Lake Geneva all alone, from early in the morning until the moon rose, keenly aware of your nearness. I read your book through with my senses refreshed and said to myself over and over that I'd never experienced a more hallowed Sunday. A feeling of purity and love never left me, and all day long nature was nothing but the mirror image of this mood. You appeared before me as a higher, a *much* higher self—but more to inspire than to shame. Thus you loomed before me, and I measured my life against this model and reflected on my many failings. I am grateful to you for very much more than a book. I was sick, and mistrusted my powers and goals. . . . Now I'm healthier and freer. . . . One of the noblest impulses, of which I knew nothing before I met you, is that of mother-love without the physical tie between mother and child; it is one of the most splendid manifestations of *caritas*. Bestow on me some of this love, my highly honored friend, and look upon me as a son who has need — oh so great a need! — of such a mother. . . .

37 TO MATHILDE TRAMPEDACH

Basel, 15 April 1876

Highly honored Fräulein, you are generous enough to forgive me — I can feel it in the mild tone of your letter, which I certainly do not deserve. I have suffered so much over my gruesome, violent way of going about things that I cannot thank you enough for this gentleness. I don't want to explain anything and I have no idea how to justify myself. But I do want to express one last wish: should you ever see my name in print or meet me again, don't think only of the fright I gave you. I beg you to believe, come what may, that I would willingly make good what I have done badly.

38 TO ERWIN ROHDE

Basel, 23 May 1876

This is a moment for us to share heartfelt joy, my dear friend, now that your work[1] is finished. . . .

I notice that you say so little about pederastic relations. Yet with the Greeks the idealizing of eros and the purer and more ardent experience of the passion of love first grew in this soil and, it seems to me, was only subsequently carried over into heterosexual love, whose refinement it prevented from taking place any sooner. That the Greeks of the classical period founded the education of their men on this passion, and, as long as they kept this practice up, looked upon heterosexual love in general with disfavor, is astonishing indeed, but appears to me to be true. . . .

[1] *The Greek Novel and Its Predecessors.*

39 TO ERWIN ROHDE

[Basel, 18 July 1876]

Best wishes, my dear and faithful friend, best wishes from the bottom of my heart. So in this year of grace 1876 you mean to build yourself a nest, just like Overbeck; still, I don't suppose your new-found happiness will draw you two away from me. My concern for you will be eased — even though I may not follow in your footsteps. After all, you needed this completely trustful soul so much, and, having found her, have been exalted. For me it's different, heaven knows (or doesn't). All this seems less essential to me — except once in a blue moon.

Perhaps there's something seriously missing in me. My needs are different. I barely know how to say this or explain it.

Last night I had an impulse to put it into verse. I'm no poet, but you'll understand me well enough.

> A wanderer breaks the spell of night
> With steady gait;
> No twisting vales or mountain peaks
> His steps abate.
> The night is fair —
> He marches on: no rest indeed
> While wond'ring where the path will lead.
> A bird's song breaks the spell of night. —
> — "Oh dear bird, what gives you the right
> To lull my brain, to stay my feet
> By pouring out heart's bittersweet
> Upon me, so that in midstreet
> I must retreat
> And try to fathom what you tweet?"

The good bird stops his song to say:
"No, wanderer, no! I greet *you* nay
With such an air!
I sing because the night is fair;
But you will have to run along
And never understand my song.
Get going, then!—
When you're far off, and only then
Will I take up my song again,
As best I can.
Good luck, you poor dear wandering man!"

Thus it came to me in the night, after receiving your letter.

40 TO LOUISE OTT[1]

Basel, 30 August 1876

My dear Frau Ott! When you left Bayreuth it was as though the light had gone with you. I had to find myself again in the dark, but I've done that now, so there's no reason why this letter should upset you.

Let us hold fast to the purity of spirit which brought us together. Let us be true to one another.

My affection for you is so much like a brother's that I could love your husband just because he is your husband. Would you believe that I think of your little Marcel ten times a day?

Shall I send you my first three *Untimely Reflections*? You really ought to know what I believe in and live for.

Don't ever lose faith in me, and help me do what I must.

Yours in purity of spirit,
Friedrich Nietzsche

[1] Mme. Ott, of Alsatian background, was a well-to-do member of Protestant Parisian society. Nietzsche appears to have fallen in love with her during these for him very disturbing and destiny-laden August days in Bayreuth, and might well have proposed to her had she not recently been married. He wrote her some half dozen brief letters between 1876 and 1882, and dedicated two poems to her.

41 TO LOUISE OTT

Basel [22 September 1876]

Dear and good friend, at first I *couldn't* write, for they were working on my eyes; and now I *shouldn't* write, for a long time to come! Still — I've read your two letters again and again, no doubt too often, but this friendship is like new wine: delightful but perhaps a bit dangerous.

For me in any case.

But also for you, when I think of what a free spirit you've run into! A man who desires nothing more than to shed daily some comforting belief, who seeks and finds his fortune in this gradual freeing of the spirit. Perhaps I *want* to be even more of a free spirit than I *can* be.

What should we do now? A spiritual *Abduction from the Seraglio*, without the Mozartian music?

Are you acquainted with the biography of Frl. von Meysenbug, entitled *Memoirs of an Idealist?*[1]

How's poor little Marcel doing with his teeth? We all have to suffer before we learn to bite properly — physically and morally. — To bite in order to nourish ourselves, of course, not for the sake of biting! . . .

[1] Malwida von Meysenbug had given Nietzsche a shorter, French version of this book, published anonymously in Basel in 1872, the year in which they first met. An expanded, three-volume German edition was published in Stuttgart in 1875–1876.

42 TO RICHARD WAGNER

Basel, 27 September 1876

Highly honored friend! . . . When I picture you in Italy it brings to mind that the inspiration to begin *Rheingold* came to you there. May it always remain for you the land of beginnings! Besides, you'll be rid of the Germans there for a time, and that seems to be necessary now and again in order to do anything worthwhile for them.

Perhaps you know that I too am going to Italy next month, but less in search of beginnings than to end my woes. These are at a peak again; it's now or never. My superiors know what they're doing in giving me a full year's leave, even though it is an enormous sacrifice for so small a community: they'd lose me in any case if they didn't offer me this way out. In the last few years, thanks to my sturdy constitution, I've swallowed pain without end, almost as if I'd been born for nothing else. To the philosophy which preaches this I've paid full tribute in practice. My neuralgia gets down to business so thoroughly, so scientifically, that it actually conducts experiments to see how much pain I can stand, and each time takes thirty hours to do the job. Every four to eight days I can count on a repetition of this research. It's a scholar's disease, you see.

But enough is enough: I mean to be healthy or be done with it. Complete quiet, mild air, good walks, dark rooms — this is what I expect from Italy. I dread having to see or hear anything there. Don't think that I'm morose; only people, not my ailments, are capable of unsettling me, and I always have about me the most helpful and considerate friends. . . .

43 TO MALWIDA VON MEYSENBUG
Rosenlauibad, 1 July 1877
. . . I've just begun a series of treatments with St. Moritz water which will keep me occupied for several weeks. . . . I still have the pleasant task of finding me a wife before fall. May the gods make me sprightly for this undertaking! Once again I had a whole year to make up my mind and wasted it. In October I'm resolved to go back to Basel again and resume my old occupation. I can't go on without the feeling that I'm *useful*, and the Baselites are the only people who let me feel that I am. My highly problematic reflecting and writing has so far always made me ill; as long as I was really a *scholar*, I was healthy. But then came that nerve-destroying music and metaphysical philosophy and concern with a thousand things which are none of my business. . . .

How much I would enjoy talking with Frau Wagner! It's always been one of my greatest pleasures, and for years I've had to do without it.

Cosima Wagner

Richard Wagner

Your motherly goodness gives you the dreary privilege of receiving letters of *lament* too!

Overbeck in no way persuaded me to go back to Basel. But my sister did. She has more sense than I do. . . .

44 TO CARL FUCHS

Rosenlauibad, end of July 1877

. . . I recall that in 1870, during a study of ancient rhythmic patterns, I was in quest of five- and seven-measure phrases and counted my way through *Meistersinger* and *Tristan*. In the process I discovered something about Wagner's own rhythmic procedures. He has such an aversion to anything mathematical, anything strictly symmetrical . . . that he is inclined to draw out four-measure phrases into five measures, six-measure phrases into seven measures. . . . At times—though this may be sacrilege—I'm reminded of the style of Bernini, who can no longer bear having even his pillars plain, but must enliven them (or so he thinks) from top to bottom with scrollwork. Among the dangerous aftereffects of Wagner, the will-to-enliven-at-any-cost strikes me as one of the worst, because quick as a flash it becomes affectation, sleight-of-hand. . . .

When you write your "Musical Letters" use as few expressions as possible from Schopenhauer's metaphysics; for I believe—pardon me! I think I *know*—that it is false, and that all writing which bears its imprint soon becomes incomprehensible. . . .

45 TO PAUL DEUSSEN

[Rosenlauibad, early August 1877]

Dear friend, how long it's taken me to thank you for the gift of your book! [*Die Elemente der Metaphysik*] . . .

You've put these last years to very good use. A strong desire to learn, an accomplished clarity, and a decided ability to communicate . . . stand out on every page of your book. For all those who wish to become acquainted with Schopenhauer, but especially for those who want to test their knowledge of him, you have provided an excellent guide. Moreover, the reader will find quite a bit of your own here, for which he should be grateful (particularly in the very difficult domain of Indian studies).

Speaking quite personally, I have one regret: that I didn't receive a book like this a number of years ago. How much more grateful I would have been to you then! But such is the fleeting nature of our convictions that, curiously enough, your book serves me as a fine collection of everything that I no longer regard as true. How sad! But I don't want to say any more about it, lest our differences cause you pain. Even when I was writing my little piece on Schopenhauer I was no longer very committed to any of his dogmas; although I still believe, as I did then, that there's a lot to learn from him. . . .

46   TO ERWIN ROHDE
[Rosenlauibad, 28 August 1877]

Dear, dear friend, how shall I put it in words? Whenever I think of you, I'm overcome by emotion. And recently when somebody wrote me that "Rohde's young wife is most charming, with a noble soul that shines forth through every feature," I even shed tears—for which I have no plausible explanation. We might ask the psychologists; they'll end up deciding it's envy, that I begrudge you your good fortune, or anger that someone has carried off my friend and hidden him God knows where, along the Rhine or in Paris, and will not yield him up again! . . .

Shall I tell you about myself? How I'm already under way two hours before the sun is in the mountains, and at it once again in the lengthening shadows of the afternoon and evening? How I've thought a lot of things through and feel so rich now, after this year finally enabled me to climb out of the old rut of having to teach and think *on tap* every day? The way I live now I can endure the worst of my afflictions (which followed me even up here), for in between them there are so many happy peaks of thought and feeling. . . .

In three days I'm going back to Basel. My sister is already there, busy with the living arrangements.

My faithful musician P. Gast is moving in, having volunteered to serve as secretary-companion.

I rather dread the coming winter; things have *got* to change. Anyone who day in and day out has only a little time for his true business, and must expend nearly all his energy on duties others could perform just as well, is not harmonious, is at odds with himself, and in the end becomes sick. . . .

47 TO REINHARD VON SEYDLITZ
Basel, 4 January 1878

. . . Yesterday Wagner sent *Parsifal* to my house. Impressions on first reading: more Liszt than Wagner, spirit of the Counter-Reformation. For me, being overly habituated to a Greek, universally human outlook, it's all too Christian, dated, narrow-minded. All sorts of bizarre psychology. No meat and far too much blood (during the Last Supper in particular things are too gory for me). I don't like hysterical females either. A good deal that's tolerable for the mind's eye will hardly be endurable on stage — picture our performers praying, trembling, their necks contorted in ecstasy. Likewise, the interior of the Grail Castle simply can't be effective on stage, any more than the wounded swan. All these fine inventions are appropriate for epic poetry and, as I say, for the mind's eye. The language sounds like it's translated from a foreign tongue. But the situations and the way they unfold — isn't that the loftiest poetry? Isn't this music at its outer limits? . . .

48 TO REINHARD VON SEYDLITZ
Basel, 13 May 1878

Dear friend, for three weeks now I've been back at the summer semester routine — and very pleased about it.

Little time for anything else! Today just a hint of what's happening. A friend will understand.

If you can know how it feels — it is something quite unique — to have declared your goal publicly for the first time,[1] a goal which no one else has, which almost no one can comprehend and for which one measly lifetime will have to suffice, then you will also know why this year, as soon as I am released from my duties, I have to have solitude. I shall want no friend, no one at all then — that's so essential. Do please accept this without further explanation. . . .

[1] Nietzsche is referring to *Human, All Too Human,* which appeared in early May.

49   TO PETER GAST

Basel, 31 May 1878

Dear friend, on Voltaire's centennial yesterday two things arrived, both of them very touching: first your letter, and then, sent anonymously from Paris, a bust of Voltaire, with a card attached saying simply: *"l'âme de Voltaire fait ses compliments à Frédéric Nietzsche."*[1]

When I think of the two men who, in addition to yourself, have shown that they are genuinely pleased with my book — Rée[2] and Burckhardt (who likes to call it "that sovereign book"),[3] I get some inkling of what caliber of people it would take for my work to have an immediate impact. But it *won't* and *can't*, much as I regret it for the admirable Schmeitzner's[4] sake. In Bayreuth the book has been placed under a sort of ban, and it seems that excommunication has been decreed for its author at the same time. Only they're trying to hang on to my friends while getting rid of me — you see, I hear a lot about what's going on behind my back. Wagner has missed a golden opportunity to show greatness of character.[5] I must not let this distort my opinion of him, or of myself.

. . . Rée says that only once before has a book afforded him such creative enjoyment — Eckermann's *Conversations with Goethe* — and that entire notebooks of reflections have already resulted. But this is just what I'd hoped for: the stimulation of creativity in others and the "increase of independence in the world" (as Burckhardt puts it).

My health is improving; I engage tirelessly in walking and solitary reflection. I take joy in the spring and am calm, like one who can no longer be so easily pushed off the track. If only I could live like this to the end! . . .

[1] The first edition of *Human, All Too Human* was dedicated to the memory of Voltaire (died 30 May 1778).

[2] The copy given Rée is inscribed: "To you it belongs — to others it will be given!" ("den andern wird's geschenkt!" carries an overtone something like: "they wouldn't take it as a gift!") Nietzsche adds: "All of my friends are now of one mind, namely that my book was written by and had its source in you. And so I congratulate you on this new paternity! Long live Réealism!"

[3] Burckhardt's remark was probably written with a dash of good-natured mockery.

[4] Ernst Schmeitzner, Nietzsche's publisher, who had taken over from E. W. Fritzsch in 1874, i.e. with the second of the *Untimely Reflections*.

[5] Cf. *Human, All Too Human*, II, Part One, aphorism 384: "Unforgivable. — You gave him an opportunity to display greatness of character, and he passed it up. He'll never forgive you that."

50 TO REINHARD VON SEYDLITZ
[Basel, 11 June 1878]

I'm delighted that one of my friends remains on such good terms with Wagner, for in view of what he has become — an old, inflexible man — I am less and less able to give him pleasure. His aspirations and mine keep drawing apart. This pains me considerably. But in the service of truth one must be prepared for any sacrifice. Besides, if he were aware of everything inside me that militates against his art and his aims, he'd think me one of his worst enemies — which as you know I'm not. . . .

51 TO MALWIDA VON MEYSENBUG

[Basel, 11 June 1878]

Who was it, do you suppose, who thought of me on May 30? . . . I was touched to the core — the destiny of this man who even after one hundred years arouses nothing but partisan reaction seemed menacingly symbolic. It is against the liberators of the spirit that people are most implacable in their hatred, most unjust in their love. Nevertheless, I want to go my way quietly and do without everything that might hinder me. The crisis of my life is at hand: if I didn't sense the enormous fertility of my new philosophy, I'd begin to feel horribly isolated. But I am *at one with myself.* . . .

52 TO CARL FUCHS

[Basel, June 1878]

. . . I feel stronger now, more committed to what counts than ever before — and ten times more mildly disposed towards people. The gist of it is that I now have the nerve to pursue wisdom itself and be a philosopher in my own right; previously I paid tribute to philosophers. A lot of gush and bliss went by the board, but what I got in exchange is much better. My metaphysical frenzy had at last reached the point where I could feel it pressing on my throat as though it would suffocate me. . . .

53 TO MATHILDE MAIER[1]

Interlaken, 15 July 1878

Most respected Fräulein, it can't be helped: I have to cause all my friends distress — precisely by speaking out at last on how I overcame my own. That metaphysical befogging of everything true and simple (reason's struggle to turn, against reason, all things into wonders and absurdities) and a correspondingly baroque art full of overexcitement and glorified extravagance — I mean Wagner's: it was these two things that finally made me ill. . . . I'm immeasurably nearer the Greeks than before. Now in every way I live striving for wisdom, whereas before I only idolized wise men. . . .

One summer[2] at Bayreuth I became fully conscious of all this. After attending the first performances I fled into the mountains, and there, in a little village in the woods, I produced the first draft of my book.[3]. . . Then, to please my sister, I returned to Bayreuth, this time with enough inner composure to suffer the insufferable—silently, in front of everybody! But now I'm shaking off what isn't really mine: people (friend and foe alike), habits, comforts, books. I shall live in solitude for years to come, until, as a philosopher of life, ripened and ready, I dare risk (as I shall doubtless require) human intercourse again.

Will you, in spite of all this, remain as true to me as you have been—or rather, will you be able to? You see, I've reached a level of honesty where I can endure only the purest of human relations. I shun half-friendships, and especially partisanships; I have no use for disciples. Let everyone be his (and her) own true follower.

[1] Frau Maier (1834–1910), from Mainz, was a mutual friend of Nietzsche's and Wagner's. An enthusiastic supporter of Bayreuth, she had asked Nietzsche's help four years earlier in organizing a sort of women's crusade on Wagner's behalf. He respectfully declined. (*Biog.* II, Part 2, pp. 556–557.)

[2] 1876.

[3] *Human, All Too Human,* which Nietzsche was then planning to call *The Ploughshare (Die Pflugschar).*

54 TO FRANZ OVERBECK

Interlaken, 3 September 1878

. . . To whom, dearest friend, would I rather unburden myself now than to you—to whom else indeed *could* I? There's a lot going on inside me; most of what comes from outside I have to repel. Loathsome letters. I've also finished reading Wagner's extremely bitter and unfortunate polemic against me in the August issue of the *Bayreuther Blätter*. It caused me pain, but not in the spot Wagner intended. . . .

55   TO CARL FUCHS

[Basel, end of summer 1878]

So you too, my dear Doctor, are having a Wagner crisis! It seems we're the first. In my book I exercised the greatest restraint in this regard, even though I'm absolutely certain of twenty points that would horrify all Wagnerians. Some day this will have to come to light. But I implore you not to act rashly. Wait until the fermenting stops; even in these matters there's a noble light wine. Don't write about Wagner now—there's so much more you've still to discover! You are fortunately independent of Bayreuth and other "movements"; what Wagner and Madame Wagner think of you should be a matter of complete indifference. Wagner himself is old and no longer has a spring to look forward to. But truth doesn't grow old and in these matters is yet to have its spring.

A unique combination of knowledge and native ability qualifies you to give us our first definitive descriptions of the individual styles of the great masters. But why not start out aphoristically, in the most concise form and with razor-sharp expressions? Some five hundred or so musical epigrams and observations, a distilling of your experience —that will bring you respect and renown.

But nothing topical and fragmentary (whether essays or letters for journals), before you've first shown yourself whole!—Forgive me if I seem forward in my counsel because of my desire to see you safe in the esteem of the reputation-makers. . . .

Nothing is further from my thoughts than to compete with such pitiful stuff as the *Bayreuther Blätter*, and, in general, to orient myself to any Bayreuth perspective. Even you still speak of a "split in our camp." What do I care about *camps* anymore?!! And to polemicize! against *Wolzogen*![1] How could you have dreamt of such a thing, my worthy Doctor? Sometimes I wonder what you think of yourself.—Once again, forgive me.

My friends are not happy with the style of the things you've published. This is because: (1) Your sentences are four times as long as they should be. (2) You affect an erudition which, though artful enough, betrays a terrible want of good taste (too many strange technical terms). (3) The main points don't come out forcefully — peripheral growths smother them; you don't do enough weeding and reworking. (4) You enjoy being clever; but the secret of a good writer is *never* to write for the subtle and the sophisticated. . . .

[1] Hans von Wolzogen (1848–1938), music critic and editor of the *Bayreuther Blätter*. In 1876 he had published a thematic guide to Wagner's *Ring of the Nibelungen*.

56 TO MARIE BAUMGARTNER[1]

[Basel, 7 May 1879]

If you're willing to give this pain-racked and soon to be train-packed hulk another half hour, then come tomorrow (Thursday) at your convenience. I've suffered *miserably*. Everything's come to a head, and I've resigned my professorship. In a few days I'm leaving Basel for good. My furniture is for sale. Saturday my sister is coming.

[1] Frau Baumgartner-Köchlin, an Alsatian, was the wife of an industrialist in Baden and the mother of Nietzsche's pupil Adolf Baumgartner (later professor of history in Basel). Nietzsche first met her in Basel in mid-November 1874, after she had written him enthusiastically about "Schopenhauer as Educator." They became good friends. Besides being helpful to Nietzsche in numerous ways, she translated into French the Schopenhauer essay in 1875 (her version was never published) and the last of the *Untimely Reflections*, "Richard Wagner in Bayreuth" in 1876 (published the following year). She died in 1897.

57 TO FRANZISKA NIETZSCHE

St. Moritz, 21 July 1879

My dearest mother, I was just about to write and ask you to find out how soon the lease expires when, with perfect timing, your letter arrived. So: I herewith formally pledge to pay seventeen and a half thalers a year (or twice that, if the entire courtyard is available) for six years. But I must have the tower room. Vegetable gardening is wholly in line with my desires, and is in no way degrading to a prospective "sage". You know that I favor a simple and natural way of living; I'm becoming more and more committed to it, and there is no other cure for my health. Some real labor which is tiring and time-consuming, but doesn't strain my head, is just what I need. Didn't my father say that some day I'd become a gardener? Admittedly I'm quite inexperienced (though not slow to learn), so you'll have to help me get my bearings.[1]

Eventually I'll need the water at Karlsbad for my abdominal problems. My stomach, now that I'm feeding myself in my room (milk, eggs, tongue, dried prunes, bread, and zwieback), is in fine shape. I still haven't been out to a restaurant.

My eyes cause me great concern. They alone are not improving — and alas cannot, according to the verdict of my three specialists. Can someone be found in Naumburg who could read to me or take dictation? . . .

[1] Nietzsche to Peter Gast, 30 September 1879: "I've rented from the city of Naumburg a small, fortresslike piece of its medieval protective wall, in order to raise *vegetables* — for six years(!!), as is customary. It's all grown over green and bushy; in one tower of the wall a long room (very ancient) is being fixed up for me to live in. I have 10 fruit trees, roses, lilies, carnations, strawberries, gooseberries, and currants. My work begins in spring, on 10 vegetable beds. — It's all my idea, and I've been very lucky" (*GBr* IV, 22). Before the end of October, Nietzsche had abandoned the entire project.

58 TO PETER GAST

[Naumburg, 5 October 1879]

. . . You won't believe how faithfully I've been putting into practice my plan to do without thinking. And with good reason, since "behind every thought lurks the devil"[1] of a furious attack of pain. The manuscript you received from St. Moritz[2] was purchased so dearly that perhaps no one who could have done otherwise would have written it at that price. Even now I shudder when I remember it, especially when I read the longer sections. All of it, save for a few lines, was conceived while walking, and outlined in pencil in six little notebooks. Reworking it was almost always torture. I had to pass up about two dozen rather lengthy trains of thought, important ones at that, because I never found time to extract them from that ghastly scrawl,—just like the summer before. And I tend to forget how my thoughts were connected. . . . Reading your transcript, I find it very difficult to understand myself. My head is so tired. . . .

. . . Again in all honesty, I regard you as better and more gifted than I am, and hence under far greater obligation. At your age I was investigating with boundless zeal the origins of an eleventh-century dictionary and the sources of Diogenes Laertius, and had no notion of myself as someone who had any right to entertain, never mind put forward, any far-ranging views of his own. Even now I feel like the most feckless fledgling. Being alone and ill has inured me somewhat to the "shamelessness" of my writings. But others must do it *all* better, my life as well as my thought. — Don't answer this.

[1] A play on an old Spanish saying, "Detrás de la Cruz está el diablo."
[2] "The Wanderer and His Shadow," the second part of *Human, All Too Human*, vol. 2.

59 TO MALWIDA VON MEYSENBUG
                    Naumburg, 14 January 1880
Although for me writing is forbidden fruit, you, whom I love and respect like an older sister, must have one more letter from me. It will no doubt be the last! This frightful and almost unremitting agony makes me hunger for the end — and judging by several indications, the cerebral *coup de grâce* is close enough at hand to make me hopeful. As far as suffering and self-denial go, I'll match the last years

of my life against those of any ascetic of any age. All the same I've made good use of these years to burnish and purify my soul, and no longer need religion or art for this purpose. (You see, I'm proud of it; in fact, my complete isolation first led me to discover my inner resources.) I believe I've finished my life's work, admittedly like one who was granted very little time. But I know I've helped many people, and given them a nudge in the direction of self-enhancement, serenity, and strength of mind. I'm writing you this as an epilogue; it should really be left for the very end. No amount of pain has been or will be able to betray me into bearing false witness to life *as I know it.*

. . . The two of us have followed stars whose light few of our contemporaries have seen. We hope for mankind, and bring ourselves as a modest offering, do we not?

Any news from the Wagners? It's three years now since I've heard from them. *They* abandoned me too; I knew long ago that Wagner, as soon as he realized that our aims had diverged, would do just that. . . . I am still grateful to him for having inspired me to strive passionately for independence of spirit. Frau Wagner, as you know, is the most appealing woman I've ever met. — But I'm totally unfit for social relations, never mind reunions. It's too late. . . .

60   TO DR. OTTO EISER[1]

[Naumburg, January 1880]

. . . My existence is a terrible burden. I'd long ago have chucked it were it not for my having done the most illuminating psychological and moral research in just this state of suffering and almost absolute renunciation. My joyous thirst for knowledge brings me to heights where I can triumph over all torment and despair. On the whole I'm happier than ever before in my life. And yet! — constant pain, a feeling much like seasickness several hours each day, a semi-paralysis which makes speaking difficult and, for a change of pace, furious seizures (the last involved three days and nights of vomiting; I lusted for death). To be unable to read! And barely able to write! No human contact! No music! . . .

My thoughts are my consolation. As I walk I scribble something now and again on a piece of paper; I don't write at my desk. Friends decipher my scratchings. . . .

[1] Otto Eiser was Nietzsche's eye specialist in Frankfurt. Nietzsche's eye and head miseries began when he was twelve, following a winter of unusually zealous studying. From his correspondence alone, we know of more than thirty physicians and physiologists whom he consulted at one time or another. (Alwin Mittasch in his appendix to *F. N.'s Naturbeflissenheit*, p. 140, lists them).

61 TO PAUL RÉE

[Naumburg, end of January 1880]

How much joy you've given me, my dear, my exceptionally dear friend! I've seen you once more, true to the memory I'd held in my heart. These six days have been like a continually pleasant drunken spree.[1]

I confess I've given up hope of seeing you again. My health is too shattered, my misery too constant. All this overcoming of self, all this endurance — what good has it ever done me? . . .

[1] Rée had visited Nietzsche in Naumburg, 15–22 January. For Christmas Peter Gast had sent Nietzsche the three-volume *Mémoires de Madame de Rémusat* (1879), containing valuable information about Napoleon's personal life. Rée read to Nietzsche extensively from these *Mémoires* during this visit.

62 TO PETER GAST

Marienbad, 18 July 1880

. . . It now *seems* to me as if I've found the right road; but something like this has to be believed, and rejected, a hundred times. . . .

Did you read that Mommsen's[1] house burned down? And

that his notes were destroyed—no doubt the most impressive research any living scholar has produced? It is said he plunged into the flames again and again, until at last, covered with burns, he had to be restrained by force. Undertakings like Mommsen's must be quite rare, since an incredible memory and an equal acuity in criticizing and ordering such materials seldom work in harmony, tending rather to conflict with each other.—When I heard this story my heart stopped beating, and even now I feel physical pain when I think about it. Is this compassion? But what do I care about Mommsen? I have no affection for him. . . .

In closing, a thought: one stops loving oneself properly when one stops loving others.[2] Which is why the latter is a very bad idea. (I speak from experience.)

[1] Theodor Mommsen (1817–1903), historian and archaeologist. Famed for his vivid portrayals of the Roman Empire's political struggles—and for his rather odd notions about distinguished Romans. Cicero he dismissed as "a journalist in the worst sense of the word," Pompey he regarded as a mere drill sergeant; Julius Caesar, on the other hand, he characterized as "the complete and perfect man." Mommsen was for many years a member of the Prussian Parliament.

[2] Cf. *The Dawn of Day,* aphorism 401: "One begins by forgetting to love others, and ends by no longer finding anything worth loving in onself."

63 TO PETER GAST

Marienbad, 20 August 1880

. . . You're made of stronger stuff than I am, and so are entitled to forge higher ideals. I for my part suffer horribly when I'm deprived of affection. Nothing, for example, can replace Wagner's, which the past few years have taken away from me. How often I dream of him, and always as he was in the time of our intimacy. There was never an ugly word between us, not even in my dreams, but very many buoyant and cheerful ones; and I don't think I ever laughed as much with anyone else. That's all over now. What's the use of my being right on many points? As if that could wipe this lost affection from my memory!—I've had similar experiences before, and presumably will again. The greatest sacrifices have been required of me by my life and thought. Even now my whole philosophy wavers after an hour's friendly conversation with a total stranger. It seems so silly to want to be right at the expense of love—and at the same time to be unable to impart what's most valuable in oneself, for fear of destroying affection.

. . . I'm living in obscurity here at the spa. The guest list has me down as "Herr Nietzsche, instructor." There are many Poles here and they—it's most extraordinary—insist on taking me for a Pole, keep greeting me in Polish, and refuse to believe me when I tell them I'm Swiss. . . .

64   TO FRANZ OVERBECK

[Genoa, November 1880]

. . . My daily battle with headaches, together with the ridiculous assortment of ills that plagues me, demands so much attentiveness that I run the risk of becoming petty-minded. But at least it serves to ballast the very general, very high-flying impulses which rule me to such a degree that without great counterweights I'd surely go mad. . . .

I want nothing more to do with the concerns of contemporary "idealism," especially the German variety. Let's all do our own work; posterity will set us in proper order anyhow, or maybe it won't. All I want is to feel free and not have to say Yes! and No!, for instance to such a true-blue idealistic little book[1] as the one enclosed. It's the last encounter I wish to have with the contemporary "German spirit," as sentimental as it is pretentious and unspeakably tasteless. You and your wife have a look at it. Then burn it and read, to cleanse yourselves of this German bombast, Plutarch's lives of Brutus and Dion. . . .

[1] Schlechta (III, 1458) suggests that this may have been Eduard von Hartmann's *Phenomenology of Moral Consciousness*, first published in 1879.

65 TO FRANZ OVERBECK

[Sils-Maria, Engadine, 23 June 1881]

... As far as Christianity is concerned, I hope you'll believe this much: in my heart I've never held it in contempt and, ever since childhood, have often struggled with myself on behalf of its ideals. In the end, to be sure, the result has always been the sheerest impossibility. . . .[1]

I no longer have the slightest idea which of my views do good, which harm.

[1]These remarks were prompted by the appearance at this time of *The Dawn of Day*. Nietzsche wrote to Gast on the same day that his copy was coming, and on 21 July added: "It occurred to me, dear friend, that for you the constant inner struggle with Christianity in my book must be strange, even distressing; but it is still the best piece of ideal life which I have become really familiar with. . . . I am after all the descendant of whole generations of Christian ministers—forgive me this narrowness!"

66 TO FRANZISKA AND ELISABETH NIETZSCHE

Sils-Maria, mid-July 1881

... I reproach myself for my foolishness in sending you only those short little cards about my health; you're no doubt getting a false impression of me. There never was anyone for whom the word "depressed" was less apt. Those who have a greater sense of my life's work and its steady progress take me to be, if not the happiest, at least the most spirited of men. There's a heavier burden on me than my illness, and I'm managing to bear this too. My appearance, by the way, is excellent: physique almost like a soldier's, thanks to constant marching; stomach and abdomen in good shape. Considering the enormous amount of work it has to do, my nervous system is splendid, an object of astonishment to me—very fine and very strong. Intense and prolonged suffering, an unsuitable profession, and the faultiest treatment haven't done it serious damage. During the past year it has even grown stronger, and thanks to that I've produced one of the boldest, noblest, and soberest books[1] ever born of human brain and heart. Even if I had taken my life in Recoaro, one of the most undaunted and clear-headed of men would have died, not a despairing one.

The pains in my head are very hard to diagnose, though as regards the scientific data needed for the purpose I know more than any doctor. So it's insulting to my scholarly pride when the two of you keep proposing new remedies and go so far as to say that I'm "ignoring my illness." Have a little more confidence in me! I've been treating myself for only two years, and when I've made mistakes it was always because I finally gave in to the eager suggestions of others. That includes the stays in Naumburg, in Marien-bad, etc. . . . So don't be angry with me if I appear to reject your love and concern. I am firmly resolved to be my own doctor from now on. . . .

Write me *good* things up here, where I'm hatching the future of mankind, and let's forget about all this petty personal affliction and worry.

[1] *The Dawn of Day,* written mostly the year before in Venice and in Genoa. The inscription on the title page from the *Rig Veda* — "There are so many dawns that have not yet come to light" — was the idea of Peter Gast, who (regularly from this time on) served as Nietzsche's copyist, editor, and first and most appreciative reader. Gast's inscription also led Nietzsche to *The Dawn of Day* (*Morgenröte*) as a more appropriate title for the book than *Ploughshare* (previously considered and rejected for *Human, All Too Human*).

 TO FRANZ OVERBECK

[Sils-Maria, 30 July 1881]

I'm amazed and delighted. I have a predecessor, and what a predecessor! I hardly knew Spinoza; sheer instinct led me to him now. It isn't only that his general tendency — to make the urge to insight one's ruling passion — is the same as mine. In five essentials of his teaching I recognize myself! This most singular and solitary thinker is closest to me on just these points: he denies freedom of the will; ends; a moral world order; non-egoism; evil. There are enormous dissimilarities, to be sure, but they're mostly due to differences in time, culture, and scientific development. In a word: my lonesomeness . . . is now at least a twosomeness.

68 TO PETER GAST

Sils-Maria, 14 August 1881

Well, my dear friend! The August sun is overhead, the year is slipping away, the mountains and forests are becoming more hushed and more peaceful. Thoughts have emerged on my horizon the likes of which I've never seen, —I won't even hint at what they are, but shall maintain my own unshakable calm. I suppose now I'll have to live a few years longer! Ah, my friend, I sometimes think that I lead a highly dangerous life, since I'm one of those machines that can burst apart. The intensity of my feelings makes me shudder and laugh. Several times I have been unable to leave my room, for the ridiculous reason that my eyes were inflamed. Why? Because I'd cried too much on my wanderings the day before. Not sentimental tears, mind you, but tears of joy, to the accompaniment of which I sang and talked nonsense, filled with a new vision far superior to that of other men.

If I couldn't derive my strength from myself, if I had to depend on the outside world for encouragement, comfort, and good cheer, where would I be! What would I be! There really were moments and even whole periods in my life (e.g. the year 1878) when a word of encouragement, a friendly squeeze of the hand would have been the ideal medicine—and precisely then I was left in the lurch by all those I'd supposed I could rely on, and who *could* have done me such kindness. Now I no longer expect it, and feel only a certain dim and dreary astonishment when, for example, I think of the letters I get: it's all so meaningless. Nothing's *happened* to anyone because of me; no one's given me any thought. It's all very decent and well-intended, what they write me, but distant, distant, distant. Even our dear

Jacob Burckhardt wrote such a meek and timorous little letter. . . .[1]

What are you doing this coming winter? I assume you'll be in Vienna. But for the winter following we should plan a reunion, even if only a brief one — for I now know very well that I'm not good company for you, and that as soon as I'm gone you are more free and productive. I care more than I can say about this — about your gaining an ever greater freedom of feeling, and an understanding that is both proud and powerful; in short, about your creating and developing in the best way possible. So I'll be happy with any solution which suits your needs. I *never* have any nasty feelings about you — you can be confident of that, dear friend! . . .

[1] Upon receiving *The Dawn of Day.*

69 TO PETER GAST

Sils-Maria, end of August 1881

What splendid news, my dear, dear friend! Above all, that you're finished![1] . . . Whenever I think of your work I feel a sense of satisfaction, and an emotion comes over me which my own "works" have never aroused. There's something about these which again and again makes me ashamed: they're the likenesses of a creature that's miserable, defective, and barely master of its most vital organs. To myself I seem, viewed as a whole, so often like the scratch marks scribbled across a piece of paper by some unknown power trying out a new pen. (Our friend Schmeitzner certainly knows how to twist the knife in this regard; all his recent letters insist that my readers don't want any more aphorisms from me.) Well you, dear friend, must not be such an aphorisman . . . your task is to show your art *whole* once more! This is what I feel when I think about you, and in this prospect I enjoy the reflected fulfillment of my own nature. You alone have given me this pleasure up

to now, and only since I've come to know your music. That's
how it is between us. . . .

[1] With *Scherz, List und Rache*, an operetta based on Goethe's work of
the same name (1790).

70   TO PAUL RÉE
                                          [Genoa, 21 March 1882]
My dear friend, how much pleasure your letters give me!
They take me off in all directions, and in the end always
back to you. . . .

Do greet that Russian girl[1] for me, if you see any sense
in it: I have a passion for this kind of soul. So much so, that
I shall very soon go on the prowl for one. Considering what
I intend to do in the next ten years, it's essential. Marriage
is an entirely different story; I could agree to two years of
it at most, and even this much only in view of what I have
to do in the next ten years.

Judging from my current experiences with Köselitz,[2] we
shall never get him to accept money from us—unless it's
in the most bourgeois form of buying and selling. I wrote
to him yesterday asking if he'd sell me and two of my friends
the *Matrimonio* score.[3] I offered him 6,000 francs, payable
in four annual installments of 1,500 francs each. I consider
this proposal quite a subtle lure.[4] As soon as he says yes
I'll let you know, and ask you to negotiate with Gersdorff. . . .

[1] Lou Salomé.
[2] Peter Gast, who was at this time particularly depressed, for professional and financial reasons, and because of his health.
[3] The piano score of Gast's major work, *The Lion of Venice,* whose text
was a reworking of the Bertati text to Cimarosa's *Il matrimonio segreto*
(1792).
[4] Gast wasn't lured. Extremely proud and fully aware of Nietzsche's own
financial circumstances, he expressed incredulity, gave Nietzsche warm
thanks for his good intentions, and firmly refused.

71 TO LOU SALOMÉ

[Naumburg, c. 10 June 1882]

From this distance, my dear friend, I cannot make out which people *have* to be told about our plans, but I think we should make sure we confide only in them. I love privacy, and want very much that you and I be spared the gossip of a whole continent. Other than that, I have such high hopes for our living together that all repercussions, essential or incidental, are of little concern to me just now. Whatever happens we'll bear it together, and together each evening we'll put our little worries behind us — agreed? . . .

Finally, in all practical matters I'm highly inexperienced. For years now I've never had to explain or justify to others anything I've done. I prefer to keep my plans secret; the whole world may talk about what I do if it wishes. But nature has given every creature its own weapons of defense — to you it gave your magnificent honesty. Pindar says somewhere, "Become what you are."

72 TO FRANZ OVERBECK

[Naumburg, summer 1882]

My dear friend, I've been sick for some time — had an extremely painful attack. Am gradually recovering. And now your letter![1] A letter like that comes once in a lifetime. I thank you from the bottom of my heart; I'll never forget this. How fortunate I am to have my plans, which would appear utterly fantastic to uninitiated eyes, received and understood in such a thoroughly friendly manner by you and your dear wife. . . .

Here at home, I'm maintaining constant silence. I'm determined to keep my sister out of it; she could only confuse things (herself first and foremost). . . .

[1] Unfortunately, this letter has been lost.

Malwida von Meysenbug

Lou von Salomé, Paul Rée, and Nietzsche

Peter Gast

Lou von Salomé

73 TO LOU SALOMÉ

[Tautenburg (Thuringia), 2 July 1882]

My dear friend, how bright the sky above me is now! Yesterday at noon it was like a birthday party around here: you said yes, the loveliest gift anyone could have given me at this moment; my sister sent cherries; Teubner[1] sent the first three proof sheets of *The Gay Science*; on top of all that, I had just finished the very last part of the manuscript, thus ending six years' work (1876–1882) — all my "free thinking." And what years! What tortures of every kind, what periods of loneliness, of disgust with life! And as a homemade remedy against all this, against life as much as death, I brewed my own potion, those ideas of mine with their little patches of unclouded sky above them. Oh dear friend, whenever I think of all this I'm deeply moved, and can't understand how it could possibly have worked out so well. I'm all full of self-pity and a feeling of victory. For it is a victory, and a total one; even my physical health has returned, I've no idea how, and everyone tells me I look younger than ever. Heaven protect me from stupidity! — But from now on, when you advise me, I'll be in good hands and need have no fear.

. . . I don't want to be lonely any more and wish to rediscover how to be human. *This* is a lesson I'll have to learn almost from scratch! . . .

[1] B. G. Teubner was Nietzsche's printer in Leipzig.

74 TO PETER GAST

Tautenburg, 13 July 1882

My dear friend, there are no words I'd rather hear from your lips than "hope" and "relaxation" — and here I come with my accursed need for editorial help, just when you should be basking in paradise.

Have you seen my innocuous little things from Messina?[1] Or have you kept silent about them out of politeness? In spite of what the woodpecker says in that last little poem, my verse-making leaves something to be desired.

But so what? Our wisdom isn't worth much if we are ashamed of our follies.

The poem called "To Suffering" was not my work. It is one of those things which completely overwhelm me. I've never yet been able to read it without tears: here is a voice I've been waiting and waiting for ever since childhood. The poem is by my friend Lou; you haven't heard about her before. She is a Russian general's daughter, twenty years old, keen as an eagle, brave as a lion, and yet a very girlish child who may well not live long. I owe her to Frl. von Meysenbug and Rée. She's visiting Rée just now; after Bayreuth she's coming here to Tautenburg, and in the fall we'll move together to Vienna. She's amazingly ripe and ready for *my* way of thinking.

Dear friend, you'll surely do us both the honor of keeping the notion of a love affair far removed from our relationship. We are *friends,* and I intend to hold this girl and her trust in me sacred. Besides, she has an unbelievably firm character and knows exactly what she wants — without consulting or caring about the world's opinion.[2]

This is for you and for no one else. . . .

[1] The "Idylls from Messina" were a half dozen poems Nietzsche wrote after his visit there in April. Although he had decided to have nothing to do with his anti-Semitic publisher Schmeitzner's literary journal, *Internationale Monatsschrift,* he couldn't resist the temptation to have his saucy verses appear in the June issue, between installments of a worshipful study of him by one Rudolf Lehmann. The poems were later revised and appended to *The Gay Science.*

[2] While largely true of her, the same can hardly be said of Nietzsche, who consulted at least Rée, Malwida, Overbeck, and his sister, and for the next two years found himself caring a great deal more than he would have wished. Along with the letter to his sister in early September, the following, to Gast on 4 August 1882, is a model of Nietzschean objectivity and detachment for this period — a calm before the storm: "One day a bird flew past me; and I, superstitious like all lonely people who are at a turning-point in their lives, thought I'd seen an eagle. Now all the world is busy proving to me how wrong I am, — and there's a proper European gossip about it. Well, who is better off — I, 'the deluded one,' as they say, who on account of this bird-call dwelt for a whole summer in a higher world of hope — or those 'whom there's no deceiving'? — And so forth. Amen." (*G Br* IV, 113–114.)

75 TO ERWIN ROHDE

Tautenburg [15 July 1882]

My dear old friend, it can't be helped; I must prepare you today for a new book of mine. You have at most four weeks' peace remaining! However, it will be my last for a number of years. For in the fall I'm going to the University of Vienna to start my student years anew, the old ones having miscarried somewhat because of a too one-sided concern with philology. . . .

This is really my only excuse for the kind of literature I've been doing since 1876: it's my homemade remedy for disgust with life. What years! What relentless pain! What psychic upheavals and solitary confinements! If I stand above it all now with the happy disposition of a conqueror, laden down with new plans (and, if I know me, face the prospect of even greater suffering and misfortune, though *ready and willing*), no one should be angry with me if I think well of my own doctoring. *Mihi ipsi scripsi* — that's how it is. And so it should be with everyone: his best for himself in his own way. That's my morality, the only one I have left. . . .

Admittedly, others could be ruined by my remedies; that's why I'm always the first to preach caution. This latest book in particular, entitled *The Gay Science,* will make many recoil in horror from me, — even you perhaps, dear old friend Rohde! There's a picture of me in it, and I know for certain it's not the one you carry in your heart.

So be patient, if only because you must see that for me it is a matter of life and death.

76 TO PETER GAST

Tautenburg, 25 July 1882

So, my dear friend, I'm to have music too![1] Good things are pouring in this summer — it's as if I had a victory to celebrate. And so I do: think how since 1876 I've been, body and soul, more of a battlefield than a human being. . . .

Your melancholy words, "always a bridesmaid, never a bride," weigh heavily on my heart. There were times when I thought the same about myself. But apart from the other ways in which we're different, I'm more easily pushed around than you.

I spent Sunday in Naumburg preparing my sister a bit more for *Parsifal*.² A remarkable thing happened to me . . . I dug out some old scores of mine and, for the first time in ages, replayed them. The identity of mood and expression was fantastic! . . . I must confess it came as a real shock to realize once again how very much alike Wagner and I are. . . . Of course you understand, dear friend, no praise for *Parsifal* is intended. What decadence! What Cagliostroism!³

¹Nietzsche is referring to the first half of the piano score of *The Lion of Venice*, which Gast had promised to send.

²She and Lou Salomé heard the first performance of *Parsifal* in Bayreuth on 26 July.

³Count Alessandro di Cagliostro (1743–1795), whose real name was Guiseppe Balsamo, was an unscrupulous Italian adventurer and alleged magician.

77 TO JACOB BURCKHARDT

Naumburg, August 1882

Now, my highly esteemed friend — or what should I call you? — please be well disposed to what I'm sending you today. For if you aren't, you'll simply scoff at this book, *The Gay Science*. It is much too personal, and everything personal is essentially comic.

For the rest, I've reached the point where I live as I think, and perhaps in the process I've also learned to really say what I think. In this matter your opinion will be my verdict. I'd be especially grateful if you would read "Sanctus Januarius" (Book IV) in one sitting to see if it comes across whole.

And my poetry? — — —

78 TO LOU SALOMÉ

Naumburg, end of August 1882

. . . In Naumburg the spirit came over me again—I set your "Hymn to Life" to music. My Parisian friend, Louise Ott, who has a wonderfully strong and expressive voice, must sing it for us one of these days.

Finally, my dear Lou, my old, deeply heartfelt plea: become what you are! First one needs to emancipate oneself from one's chains, and then one must free oneself from this emancipation. Each of us, though doubtless in very different ways, has to suffer from chain fever, even after he's broken his chains. . . .

79 TO ELISABETH NIETZSCHE

Naumburg, early September 1882

. . . If I could only give you some idea of the cheerful self-confidence which inspired me this summer. *Everything* worked out well, often unexpectedly, just when I thought things had gone wrong. Lou is very content also (she's hard at work and knee-deep in books). What means a great deal to me is that she has converted Rée to a key conception of mine (as he himself reports); it's radically changing the foundations of his book. He wrote yesterday: "Lou has certainly grown a few inches in Tautenburg."

It distresses me to hear that you are still suffering from the after-effects of those scenes, which I'd so willingly have spared you. Look at it this way: the excitement brought out in the open what might otherwise have long remained buried, namely that Lou had a rather low opinion of me and mistrusted me somewhat; and when I reflect more carefully on the circumstances in which we met, she may have been quite justified (taking into account the effect of several careless remarks by friend Rée). But now she undoubtedly thinks better of me—and surely that's the main thing, isn't it, my dear sister? . . .

Perhaps I've already dwelt too long on this point. I thank you once more with all my heart for everything you did for me this summer; and I can perceive your sisterly benevolence just as clearly in those matters where we couldn't see eye to eye. Indeed, who can afford to have anything to do with such an antimoral philosopher! But two things are unconditionally forbidden me by my way of thought: (1) remorse, (2) moral indignation.

Be nice again, dear Lama!

80 TO FRANZ OVERBECK

[Leipzig, early September 1882]

My dear friend, here I am back in Leipzig, the old city of books, in order to read a few before I take off again. It seems my German winter campaign just won't work: I need my weather *clear* in every way. Oh yes, Germany's cloudy skies have character, something like the way the music of *Parsifal* has character—a bad one. . . .

The most profitable of all my activities this summer were my conversations with Lou. Our minds and tastes are profoundly alike, and yet there are so many sharp contrasts that we are the most instructive subjects of study for each other. I've never met anyone else who was able to glean so many objective insights from personal experience. . . . Her health will not hold out beyond six or seven years, I'm afraid. . . .

Unfortunately my sister became Lou's mortal enemy. She was full of moral indignation from beginning to end, and claims she now knows what my philosophy is all about. She wrote my mother that in Tautenburg she saw my philosophy in action and was horrified; that I love evil whereas she loves the good; that if she were Catholic she'd enter a convent and do penance for all the trouble I will cause. In short, I now have Naumburger "virtue" against me; there's a real rift between us. At one point my mother herself said something so rash that I had my trunks packed and left for Leipzig early the next morning. My sister (who refused to come to Naumburg while I was there and is still in Tautenburg) quotes with irony: "Thus began Zarathustra's descent."[1] —In fact, it is the beginning of everything. . . .

[1] This is the last line of "Sanctus Januarius," Book IV of *The Gay Science*.

81 TO PAUL RÉE

Santa Margherita [end of November 1882]

But my dear, dear friend, I thought you'd feel just the opposite and be secretly glad to be rid of me for a while! There were a hundred moments this year . . . when I felt that you are paying too high a price for our friendship. I've already had much too great a share of your Roman discovery (I mean Lou)—and it seemed to me all along, especially in Leipzig, that you had a right to treat me a bit coldly.

Think as well as possible of me, dearest friend, and please ask Lou to do the same. I'm deeply devoted to both of you—and believe I've proved this more by my absence than by my presence.

Proximity makes one insatiable, and after all I'm a demanding person as it is.

We'll see each other again from time to time, won't we? Don't forget that as of this year I'm suddenly low on affection, and hence very much in need of it.

Write me in full detail about what currently concerns us most,—what "has come between us," as you say.

82 TO LOU SALOMÉ AND PAUL RÉE

[Santa Margherita, mid-December 1882]

Lou and Rée, my dears! Don't be too upset by my fits of "megalomania" or "wounded vanity." And even if some emotional disturbance should happen to drive me to suicide, there wouldn't be all that much to mourn. Why should my fantasies concern you? (Even my "truths" haven't concerned you up to now). Do bear in mind, you two, that at bottom I'm sick in the head and half-insane, completely confused by long isolation.

I've arrived at this reasonable (or so I believe) insight into how matters stand after having, in desperation, taken an enormous quantity of opium. But instead of making me lose my senses, it seems to have finally brought me to them. . . .

Friend Rée, ask Lou to forgive me for everything. She'll surely grant me another opportunity to forgive her too—I haven't so far.

It's much harder to forgive one's friends than one's enemies.[1]

[1]The remainder of this letter, after a few words that begin a new paragraph, is lost.

83   TO HANS VON BÜLOW

[Santa Margherita, December 1882]

. . . For years now I've lived somewhat too close to death and, what's worse, to pain. I seem designed for lengthy torment and skewering over a slow flame, and don't even know enough to lose my mind in the process. I'll say nothing about the dangerous nature of my passions; but my new way of thinking and perceiving, which has been reflected in my books for the past six years, has kept me alive and has almost cured me. What do I care if my friends maintain that my current "freespiritedness" is eccentric, something desperately forced through against my own natural inclinations? All right, it may be a "second" nature; but I shall yet show that only with this second nature did I come into proper possession of my first. . . .

84   TO FRANZ OVERBECK

[Rapallo, 25 December 1882]

Dear friend, perhaps you didn't get my last letter at all? This latest morsel of my life has been the hardest I've so far had to chew, and I may yet choke on it. The humiliating memories of the past summer have been as agonizing as a fit of madness. My allusions to it in Basel and in my last letter always concealed the most essential thing. It has to do with a war of conflicting impulses which is more than I can master, though I strain all the fibers of my self-control.

I've lived too long in isolation, "off my own fat," so that now I am particularly fit to be broken on the wheel of my passions. If only I could sleep! But the heaviest doses of my sleeping potions help no more than my six to eight hour walks.

If I don't discover the alchemist's device for making gold even out of this—crap, I'm lost. Here I have the most splendid opportunity to prove that for me "every experience is instructive, each day holy, and all men divine."[1]

All men divine.

I'm feeling terribly suspicious just now. In everything I hear, I detect a note of contempt. Most recently in a letter from Rohde. I'd swear that if we hadn't happened to be friends at one time, he'd look upon me and my aims with utter contempt.

Yesterday I even broke off correspondence with my mother. . . .

My relationship with Lou is in its last and most painful throes—at least so I think today. Later, if there is a later, I'll say something about that too. Pity, my dear friend, is a kind of hell, regardless of what Schopenhauer's disciples may say. . . .

You and your shrewd and admirable wife are just about my last strip of solid ground. Curious!

[1] From Ralph Waldo Emerson's essay "History." ("To the poet, to the philosopher, to the saint, all things are friendly and sacred, all events profitable, all days holy, all men divine.")

85 TO FRANZ OVERBECK
[Rapallo, received 11 February 1883]
. . . I won't conceal it from you: I'm in a bad way. Darkness has closed in on me again. . . . For a short time I was completely in my element, basking in my light. And now it's over. I believe I'm surely done for unless something (I have no idea what) happens. Like somebody hauling me out of Europe. I see myself now—me with my physiological

turn of mind — as the victim of an atmospheric disturbance to which all Europe lies exposed. How can I help it if I have an extra sense, and therefore a new and terrible source of suffering? Just to think of it like that eases things; I don't have to indict my fellow men as causes of my misery. Though I could! And do, only too often! Everything I've hinted at in my letters is only peripheral. I have such a bulging bag of painful, horrible memories to carry!

Thus I haven't been able to forget, even for an hour, that my mother called me a disgrace to the grave of my father.

... I've always been prone to the cruelest accidents. Or rather, I'm the one who's made horrors out of all accidents. . . .

86 TO PETER GAST
Rapallo, 19 February 1883

... The incredible burden of the weather (even old Etna is beginning to belch) transformed itself into thoughts and feelings of frightful intensity. And out of my sudden release from this burden, in the wake of ten absolutely bright and bracing January days, *Zarathustra* was born, the most emancipated of my offspring. Teubner has already started printing. I did the transcribing myself. —Schmeitzner reports that during the past year all my books have sold better, and there are many other signs of a growing interest. . . .

Forgive me for this babbling; you know what else is on my mind and in my heart just now. For several days I was violently ill. . . . I'm better now, and I even think that Wagner's death is the most substantial relief I could have been granted. It was hard having to be, for six years, the opponent of the man I had respected most — I'm not crudely enough constructed for that. Toward the end it was a Wagner grown old whom I had to fight; as for the true Wagner, I still expect to become in good measure his heir (regardless of what Malwida says). Last summer I found that he had taken away from me everyone at all worth influencing

in Germany and had begun drawing them into the mud-
dled, desertlike malignancy of his old age. . . .[1]

[1]Wagner, who had died on 13 February, was very much on Nietzsche's
mind during the next months. To Gast on 27 April, reminiscing about the
summer of 1869, when the last part of *Siegfried* was finished, Nietzsche
wrote: "At that time we loved one another and wanted the world for each
other — it was really a deep love, without mental reservations."

 TO FRANZ OVERBECK
[Rapallo, 22 February 1883]
Dear friend, it's going *very* badly. My health is back to
where it was three years ago. Everything is wrecked — my
stomach can't even stand sleeping potions any more. . . .

I'm off to seek health along the trail previously taken,
but in utter seclusion. My mistake last year was *abandoning* my isolation. Spending all my time with ideal images
and events has made me so sensitive that I suffer incredibly in the company of contemporaries, and end up being
hard and unjust. . . .

What a life! And I'm the great affirmer of life!! . . .

88 TO PAUL DEUSSEN
[Genoa, 16 March 1883]
That's fine, dear old friend, that's the way to go about
it! . . . Only a man of many talents could have revealed the
teaching of the Vedânta to us Europeans.[1] And I find it
commendable that you have not forgotten how to work
hard. . . . Heaven knows, without honest industry nothing
but weeds grow in the finest soil. Indeed, even the best artist should not put himself above the craftsman. I hate that
riff-raff which has no use for good workmanship, and ap-
preciates only the intellect of a dilettante.

I'm very pleased to have this introduction to the classical
expression of the mode of thought I find most alien — this is

what your book has given me. It brings everything I sus-
pected about this way of thinking so ingenuously to light; I
read page after page with utter malice. You couldn't hope
for a more grateful reader, dear friend!

It so happens that right now a manifesto of mine[2] is being
printed which says Yes wherever your book says No, and
just about as eloquently. This amuses me no end — but perhaps you'd find it offensive. I haven't made up my mind
yet whether to send it. To write your book you *couldn't*
think about things as I do; and your book *had* to be written.
Ergo — —

[1]Deussen's *The System of the Vedânta* had just arrived.
[2]*Zarathustra*, I.

89   TO FRANZ OVERBECK
                        [Genoa, received 24 March 1883]
My dear friend . . . I've lost interest in everything. Deep
down, an unyielding black melancholy. And weariness too.
Most of the time I'm in bed. . . . The worst of it is, I no
longer see why I should live for even half a year more.
Everything is boring, painful, *dégoûtant*. I've suffered too
much and sacrificed too much; I feel so incomplete, so inexpressibly conscious of having bungled and botched my whole
creative life. It's all hopeless. I won't do anything worthwhile again. Why do anything any more!

That reminds me of my latest folly. I mean *Zarathustra*. . . . I'm curious to know whether it has any merit whatsoever. I myself am incapable of judgment this winter and
could be grotesquely mistaken about such things. Besides,
I've heard and seen nothing of the book, even though I
insisted that they print it as quickly as possible. Day after
day, only my general weariness has kept me from wiring
that the whole business be stopped. I've been waiting more
than four weeks for the proofs. It's indecent to treat me like
this — but then who is still decent to me? So I'll just put up
with it. . . .

90 TO JACOB BURCKHARDT

[Rome, June 1883]

Most worthy Professor, all I miss now is a conversation with you. . . . As for the little book[1] enclosed, I'll say only that for everyone there comes a time when he must pour out his heart, and that the good this does him is so great that he can scarcely appreciate how much it pains everyone else.

I have a hunch that I'll hurt you even more this time than ever before—but also that you, who've always been good to me, will from now on be even kinder.

You know, don't you, how much I love and respect you?

[1] *Zarathustra*, I.

91 TO CARL VON GERSDORFF

Sils-Maria [28 June 1883]

. . . I've chosen to go through a long and difficult spiritual discipline. Not everyone could have done it. . . .

The time for silence is over. My *Zarathustra*, which will be sent to you within a few weeks, may give you a hint of how high my will has soared. Don't be put off by the mythic style of the book: my entire philosophy is behind those homey and unusual words, and I have never been more serious. It is a beginning at self-disclosure—nothing more! I know perfectly well that there's no one alive who could write anything like *Zarathustra*.

Dear old friend, I'm back in the Upper Engadine again, for the third time, and once more I feel that here and nowhere else is my true home and spawning-ground. Oh, what still lies buried in me, waiting to become word and form! For hearing my innermost voices, it can never be too peaceful and high and lonely.

I wish I had enough money to build myself a kind of glorified dog kennel here. I have in mind a wooden house with two rooms, on a peninsula jutting out into Lake Sils, where a Roman fortress once stood. For I'm beginning to find it impossible to live in these farmhouses any longer. The rooms are low and cheerless, and there's always some sort of disturbance. But the people of Sils-Maria are friendly, and I respect them. . . .

Don't forsake me — we are old comrades and have been through a lot together.

92 TO MALWIDA VON MEYSENBUG

Sils-Maria, August 1883

. . . The summer has been bad, and it's not getting better. Last year's nasty business has come crashing down on me all over again. I've had to hear so much about it that it has changed my splendid solitude with nature into a virtual hell. Judging by everything I've now learned — much too late — those two persons Rée and Lou aren't fit to lick the soles of my boots. (Forgive this all too masculine image!) It's a great misfortune that this Rée, a liar and sneaking slanderer from the word go, ever crossed my path. . . . I haven't forgotten how furious I was in 1876 when I heard that he would be coming along to stay with you in Sorrento. And here, two years ago, the rage returned: I became ill when my sister wrote that he wanted to come up here. One should have more trust in one's instincts, including one's instincts of *repugnance*. But that Schopenhauerian "pity" has always caused the greatest mischief in my life — so I've every reason to favor moral philosophies which ascribe a few *other* motives to moral conduct, and don't try to reduce all human excellence to "fellow-feeling." For this isn't just an effeminacy at which every high-minded Hellene would have laughed, but a serious practical danger. One should make one's own ideal of mankind prevail, and overpower one's fellow men as well as oneself with it — that's acting creatively! But this requires keeping a tight rein on your sympathy, and treating what's contrary to your ideal (e.g. riff-raff like L. and R.) as an enemy.

As you can see, I'm preaching to myself — but merely to arrive at this piece of pennywisdom almost cost me my life. I should have spent the summer with you and your wonderful friends. But now it's too late.

93 TO PETER GAST

Sils-Maria, late August 1883

. . . Yesterday the proof sheets of *Zarathustra,* II came from Naumann. . . .

Based on a pretty accurate estimate of the over-all design I'd say that, with two hundred pages completed, I'm halfway through. If I bring it off (the first two parts *appear* to have succeeded, in spite of the terrible antagonism I carry about in my heart for the whole Zarathustra image) I'll have a huge feast and die of joy. — Sorry!

Had I been gay and lighthearted all year, artistic reasons would probably have led me to choose darker and harsher colors for the first two parts, considering how it all ends. But this year the tonic of gay and cheerful colors was necessary for life; and so in the second part I made my leaps almost like a buffoon. It is incredibly full of detail which, because it is drawn from what *I've* seen and suffered, only I can understand. Some pages seem to be almost bleeding. . . .

94 TO FRANZ OVERBECK

[Sils-Maria, received 28 August 1883]

(This letter is for you alone.)

Dear friend, our separation cast me back into the deepest melancholy, and all the way home I couldn't rid myself of black, evil feelings. Among them a genuine hatred of my sister, who for a whole year now, by being silent at the wrong time and by chattering at the wrong time, has ruined my finest victory over myself — so that I've ended up prey to relentless thoughts of revenge, just when my innermost way of thinking has repudiated such feelings. This conflict within me takes me step by step nearer to insanity*. . . . My reconciliation with her may have been the most disastrous phase of the whole affair. I now see that this led her to believe she was justified in her vindictiveness toward Fräulein Salomé.

. . . Enclosed is the first public response to *Zarathustra,* I; strange to say, it was written in prison. I'm pleased that

my very first reader[1] has some idea of what it's all about —
the "Antichrist" promised us long ago. Since Voltaire
there's been no such assault on Christianity; and frankly,
even he had no idea that one could attack it like this. . . .

*Couldn't you perhaps bring this aspect of the matter forcibly home to
my sister? [Nietzsche's note.]

[1] To Peter Gast two days earlier, Nietzsche had described this "first
reader" as a Christian and an anti-Semite, but had not identified him further. Gast's footnote to the letter (*GBr* IV, 469) indicates that he hasn't
found out who the man was either. Commenting on Nietzsche's very similar comparison between himself and Voltaire in this letter, Gast adds:
"The men of the Enlightenment did battle with Christianity's myth, cult,
and clergy, and regarded Christian morality as unassailable; Nietzsche
by contrast attacks the morality of Christendom, and does so for biological
reasons: because of the stunting effect it has on mankind" (*ibid*).

95 TO ERWIN ROHDE

[Nice, 22 February 1884]

My dear old friend, I don't know what brought it on, but
when I read your last letter, especially when I saw that
charming picture of your children, I felt as though you
were holding my hand and looking at me mournfully, as if
to say: "How can it be that we have so little in common
now, that we live in such different worlds? Yet at one
time— —"

And that's how it is, my friend, with everyone I care
about: it's all over, past history, merely a matter of being
considerate. We still get together. We talk, so as not to be
silent. We write letters, so as not to be silent. But the truth
can be seen in their eyes, which say to me (I hear it well
enough): "Nietzsche, you are now all alone." . . .

The three acts of my *Zarathustra* are finished (you have
the first; the other two I hope to be able to send you in four
to six weeks). It is a kind of abyss of the future — horrible,
above all in its rapture. Everything in it is me alone, without prototype, parallel, or precedent; anyone who ever *lived*
in it would come back to the world a different man.

. . . I fancy that I've now brought the German language to perfection. After Luther and Goethe there was still a third step to take. See for yourself, old bosom friend, if power, suppleness, and melody have ever before been blended like this in one language. . . . I write a stronger, manlier line than Goethe, without falling prey, as Luther did, to coarseness. My style is a dance; it plays with all sorts of symmetries, only to leap over and scoff at them. (This applies even to the choice of vowels.)

— Forgive me. I wouldn't think of making a confession like this to anyone else. But you did once say — you were the only one, I believe — how much you liked my style. . . .

Oh my friend, what a wild, secluded life I lead! So alone, alone. So without "children"!

 TO MALWIDA VON MEYSENBUG

[Venice, late April 1884[1]]

By now, my highly esteemed friend, the last two parts of *Zarathustra* are hopefully in your hands — at least I told my publisher to see to it a long time ago. For a present like this, gratitude may not be entirely appropriate. I demand a readjustment of our most precious and most venerated sentiments, and much more than a readjustment! Who knows how many generations it will take to produce a few men who can fully appreciate what I've done? And I'm appalled by the thought of all the unqualified and wholly unsuitable types who will some day appeal to my authority. But this is the torment of every great teacher of mankind: he knows that he has as much chance of becoming its curse as its blessing. I myself will do what I can to ward off at least the crudest misunderstandings. Now that I've built this vestibule for my philosophy, I must get back to work and not tire until the main structure stands finished before me. . . .

But this loneliness, ever since childhood! This reserve, in the most intimate relationships! Even kindness can no longer reach me. In Nice, during Fräulein Schirnhofer's visit, I did often think of you with genuine gratitude, for

I realized that you meant to be kind. Actually, it was a visit at the right time, a pleasant and profitable one (especially since no interfering, conceited goose was present — sorry, I was referring to my sister!). But basically I think that no one can help me overcome this deep-rooted feeling of being alone. I've never found anyone I can talk to the way I talk with myself. — Forgive me for such a confession, my revered friend. . . .

I'm angry with myself for the *inhuman* letter I sent you last summer; that unspeakably nasty turmoil made me downright ill. Meanwhile the situation has changed: I have broken with my sister completely. For heaven's sake don't dream of trying to intercede; between a vengeful anti-Semitic goose and me there can be no reconciliation. Anyway, I'm being as tolerant as I can, since I know what can be said in defense of my sister and what lies behind her so abusive and shameful behavior toward me: — love. It is absolutely necessary that she set sail for Paraguay as soon as possible.

Later, much later, she'll come to realize all by herself how much harm she did me during the most decisive period of my life with these incessant dirty-minded insinuations about my character (the business has been going on for two years!). I'm also left with the very awkward task of trying to make some amends to Dr. Rée and Frl. Salomé for what my sister has done. . . . She reduces so rich and rare a creature as Lou to "falseness and sensuality"; she sees in Dr. Rée and her nothing but two "scoundrels," — this outrages my sense of justice, whatever good reasons I may have to feel deeply insulted by them both. I found it most instructive that my sister ended up treating me with the same blind suspiciousness with which she treated Frl. S.; only then did it occur to me that all the bad things I've ever believed about Frl. S. went back to that squabble which took place before I got to know her better. My sister was capable of totally misunderstanding the situation. She is devoid of all psychological insight. Heaven protect her lest one of Dr. Förster's enemies become talkative about *him* in her presence!

Once more I beg forgiveness for having brought this old business up again. I did it only to tell you that you mustn't let your own feelings be influenced by that loathsome letter I wrote you this past summer. Exceptional people like Frl. Salomé deserve, especially when they're so young, all the indulgence and sympathy we can give them. And even if I am for various reasons not yet ready to welcome another overture from her, I do want, should things get really desperate for the girl, to ignore all personal considerations. Repeated experience has made me understand only too well how easily I could fall into just that sort of disrepute myself—deserved *and* undeserved, as always seems to be the case with such people.

¹Fragments of this letter, with a plausible beginning and end, first appeared as Nr. 379 in *GBr* V (1909)—the edition put out by Nietzsche's sister—addressed to her and omitting all passages unfavorable to her. Karl Schlechta and Wilhelm Hoppe discovered a copy of the letter Nietzsche had actually written, to Malwida, in the Archive during the thirties. We have used the text as found in Schlechta, III, 1420–1422. The three omissions are minor.

97 TO FRANZ OVERBECK

[Venice, received 2 May, 1884]

My dear friend Overbeck, it's really wonderful that we've not become estranged these last years, not even, as it seems, because of Zarathustra. I've never had any illusions that I would be other than very much alone around my fortieth year. And I also know that many bad things are still in store for me. I'll soon learn how dearly one pays for reaching—to use the foolish and false language of the ambitious—"for the highest crowns."

Meanwhile I want to make good use of the position I've achieved: I'm now very likely the most independent man in Europe. My aims and tasks are more comprehensive than anyone else's. . . .

With respect to the practical side of life I beg of you, my tried and true friend, to go on helping me maintain just one thing: the greatest possible independence and freedom from personal concerns. I think you know what Zarathustra's urging "Become hard!" means for me in particular. My tendency to do justice to everyone, and to treat with the greatest gentleness precisely what is most hostile to me, is developed to excess. This invites one danger after another, not only for me but for my task. Here indeed I need hardening and, for disciplinary reasons, an occasional bit of cruelty.

Forgive me! It doesn't always sound good when one speaks of oneself; it doesn't always smell good either.

 TO MALWIDA VON MEYSENBUG

Venice, May 1884

. . . It has now become extremely difficult to give me help; more and more, I consider it unlikely that I'll meet anyone who can. Almost every time I've entertained such hopes, it's turned out that *I* was the one who had to pitch in. But I have no time for that now. My task is enormous, my determination no less so. What I want, my son Zarathustra won't tell you. But he'll challenge you to figure it out, and perhaps you can. This much is certain: I wish to force mankind to decisions which will determine its entire future — and it may yet happen that one day whole millennia will make their most solemn vows in my name. . . .

 TO PETER GAST

Sils-Maria, 2 September 1884

. . . Here, without a stove, chilled to the marrow, my hands blue, I'll hardly be able to stand it much longer. . . .

I've managed to get the major task I set myself this summer more or less done. The next six years will go toward filling in an outline I've made of my "philosophy." It looks promising. At the moment, *Zarathustra's* value is entirely personal. For me, it is "devotional literature." For everyone else, it is obscure, mysterious, and ridiculous.

Heinrich von Stein (a splendid specimen of a man, whose company has given me real pleasure) told me candidly that of said *Zarathustra* he understood "twelve sentences and no more." I found that very comforting. . . .

My health is quite shaky; in Venice it was better, in Nice better still. One day in ten is a *good* one; that's par for my course, the devil take it!

No one to read to me! Every evening, I sit despondently in my low-ceilinged room, rattling with frost, awaiting, for three or four hours, permission to go to bed.

Today I'm being deserted by my favorite acquaintance of the summer, my neighbor at table, Frl. von Mansuroff, *dame d'honneur* of the Russian Empress. How much we had to say to each other—it's such a pity she's leaving. Just think, a genuine pupil of Chopin, full of love and admiration for this "as proud as he was unassuming" man! . . .

100   TO FRANZISKA NIETZSCHE
Zurich, 4 October 1884

My dear mother, by now you've surely heard that your children are behaving again and are in the best of spirits. I can't tell yet how long we'll stay together, though; the work I have planned will soon drive me back into seclusion come what may. Anyhow, the clubfoot I drag about with me, my 104 kilos of books, won't let me fly too far from here.

So for this year *our* reunion is out of the question; I do hope this won't be hard on you.

I was very grateful for the good intentions you expressed in your last letter about having me tour the world in more stately attire. To tell the truth I am pretty bad about such things and, because of my many changes of location, a bit too shabby, rather like a mountain sheep. . . .

101 TO CARL FUCHS

Nice [Winter 1884–1885]

Please believe, even without written testimony (something which my eyes allow less and less each year), that it would be difficult for anyone to follow your subtle investigations with greater interest than I do. If only "interest" were enough! But I lack knowledge and ability in all those areas in which your remarkably many-sided talents lie. Above all, years go by in which no one plays music for me, myself included. The last work I made thoroughly mine was Bizet's *Carmen* — and this not without a number of reservations, some quite unpardonable, about German music (which I put in almost the same category as German philosophy). . . . Rhythmic ambiguity to the point where you no longer know, or are even supposed to know, which end is which can undoubtedly achieve wondrous effects — *Tristan* is full of them — but as characteristic of an entire art it is and always will be a sign of dissolution. The part lords it over the whole, the phrase over the melody, the moment over the time-flow (*tempo* as well); pathos rules ethos (character, style, or whatever), *esprit* dominates "meaning." Sorry! What I think I detect here is a change of perspective: you see the particular much too sharply, while the whole is much too blurred — and you actually prefer this sort of optics, above all you have the *talent* for it! But this is *décadence,* a word which for us, it goes without saying, is meant not to condemn but only to describe. . . .

102 TO CARL VON GERSDORFF

Nice, 12 February 1885

My dear old friend, I live so out of the way and hear nothing about you any more. But this year, because of family matters, I have to get back to Germany again. I think we two should work out a little rendezvous, perhaps in Leipzig.

Today, not without some misgivings, I want to tell you something which carries with it a question for you. There is a fourth (last) part to *Zarathustra,* a sort of sublime finale, which is not intended for the public at all (forgive me, but in this context the words "public" and "publish" sound rather like "whorehouse" and "slut"). But it must be printed now: twenty copies for me and my friends, to be used with the greatest discretion. The cost (at C. G. Naumann's in Leipzig, who printed the preceding parts) can't be very great. But I myself, because of the [-----] of my publisher, am worse off than ever; he owes me 6,000 francs, and my lawyer tells me that it would be almost impossible to win a suit. In other words, I am forty years old, and have yet to earn a penny from all my writings. . . .

But I'll say no more. Send me your answer here, my dear old friend, as soon as possible — but a candid answer. One can be as open with me as with "the good Lord" (assuming he exists). . . .

103 TO MALWIDA VON MEYSENBUG

Nice, 13 March 1885

. . . All winter long there was a German around who "admires" me.[1] Thank heaven he's gone! He was boring, and I was forced to keep so much concealed from him. Oh, the moral tartuffery of all these dear Germans! If you could just promise me an Abbé Galiani[2] in Rome: there's a man after my taste. Or a Stendhal.

Last fall, out of conscientiousness and curiosity both, I made an effort to see where I now stand vis-à-vis Wagner's music. How I loathe this cloudy, sultry, above all histrionic and pretentious stuff! . . . It's the work of an aborted musician and man, but of a *great actor.* . . . Poor Stein — he even takes Wagner for a philosopher!

Why do I speak of this? Only to give you some idea of what's going on. How laughable it is that I am mistaken for the former Basel Professor Dr. Friedrich Nietzsche. The devil take him! What has that gentleman got to do with me? . . .

I don't like this coast, and I despise Nice, but in winter it has the driest air in Europe.

[1]The German-Italian Paul Lanzky, then in his mid-thirties, wealthy, and the owner of some property in the 3,000-foot-high spa Vallombrosa. This talented, good-natured man spontaneously called Nietzsche "Meister", offered him the use of this property as a sanctuary, and wrote four works whose very titles bear the Nietzschean imprint: *On the Path of Dionysus* (1895), *Sunset (Abendröte,* 1897), *Aphorisms of a Hermit* (1897), and *Amor Fati* (1904), a volume of poetry dedicated to Nietzsche.

[2]Ferdinando Galiani (1728–1787), Italian economist and wit, was educated for a career in the Church. He made some important contributions, from a mercantilist orientation, to the theory of international trade. Nietzsche's copy of Galiani's *Lettres à Madame d'Epinay, Voltaire, Diderot, Grimm, . . .* (2 vols., Paris, 1882) is extensively marked.

104 TO FRANZISKA AND ELISABETH NIETZSCHE
Nice, 21 March 1885

. . . Poor Gast had as bad a time in Zurich as I did (for about ten years of my youth!) in Basel. The climate of such cities makes creative work impossible; constantly tormented by this, we become ill. Basel was disastrous for me. Even now I still suffer, as I always shall, from its dreadful aftereffects.

One is punished good and proper for his ignorance. If only I had worked on things like medical and climatic problems, instead of on Theognis and Diogenes Laertius, I wouldn't be half dead now.

And so one loses his youth, is already past forty, and has barely begun to discover what's essential to him, what he should have found at least twenty years earlier.

You see, I'm more cheerful again, no doubt mainly because Herr Lanzky has gone. A most estimable man, and very devoted to me — but so what? He was the embodiment of what I call "overcast skies," "German weather." Actually, there's no one living now whom I could care much about; the people I really like are long dead, e.g. Abbé Galiani or Henri Beyle[1] or Montaigne.

I'm uneasy about my sister's future. I don't quite believe in Dr. Förster's return to Paraguay. Europe isn't really all that small, and even if one doesn't wish to live in Germany (on this point he and I agree), it is by no means necessary to go that far off. Admittedly I've as yet managed to mount little enthusiasm for "the Germanic essence," and even less for keeping this "glorious" race pure. On the contrary, on the contrary. . . .

¹Stendhal.

105 TO ELISABETH NIETZSCHE
Venice, April 1885

My dear, dear Lama, I really find it all quite amazing — for example that without further ado you're keeping company with a strange man and even want to wander off into the wide wide world. . . . I'll send you my colorfully bound personal copy of *Zarathustra;* you can set it up in some primeval American forest, as a fetish. . . .

Your proposals for the future resonated rather nicely inside me; I don't know how to thank you enough for the concern they express. But perhaps all concern for my future should be set aside for good. Life is still bearable in the morning, but rarely in the afternoon or evening. Besides, I'd venture to say that I've done enough, under adverse conditions, to be able to break camp with honor. I'm becoming too blind to read or write much more. Almost every day I have enough inspiration to provide German professors with material for two thick volumes. But I have no one for whom this stuff is suited. So much of it is forbidden fruit; it does others harm. I confess I'd very much like to give a lecture now and again, a quite proper and decent one, in the role of a moralist and distinguished "educator" who is nobody's fool. But students are so dumb, and professors even dumber. . . .

Gersdorff is coming to Switzerland this summer with his

sick wife. Lanzky, to my great astonishment, wrote me a long letter of thanks here recently; he is a changed man, and I'm supposed to be responsible! Perhaps this winter's efforts weren't quite as futile as others have been.

The Academic Society in Basel has renewed the 1,000 fr. pension for another three years, and the University Regents have again awarded me the 1,000 frs. from the Heusler Fund. The state grant of 1,000 frs. lapses at the end of the year (*not* in June), and surely won't be renewed. That's the "state of affairs."

. . . All those who gush over the "emancipation of women" have very slowly discovered that I'm their *bête noire*. In Zurich the coeds are furious with me. *At last*! And how many such "at lasts" have I to look forward to? . . .

106 TO FRANZ OVERBECK

Sils-Maria, 2 July 1885[1]

. . . I've been dictating almost every day for two or three hours. But my "philosophy"—if I have the right to call what tortures me to the very roots of my being by that name—is no longer communicable, at least not by means of print. . . . Besides, our age is endlessly superficial, and I'm often ashamed of myself for having already said so much publicly which at *no* time, even in far worthier and profounder ages, would have been appropriate for "public" consumption. This century's shamelessly "free press" is enough to ruin anyone's instincts and good taste. My models are Dante and Spinoza; they knew better how to come to terms with their solitary lot. To be sure, their way of thought, unlike mine, made solitude bearable. Indeed, nobody who had any sort of "God" to keep him company ever reached my level of loneliness. My life is now governed by the wish that things are *not* as I see them, and that someone will refute my "truths.". . .

[1] The source for this letter is *BNO* #231, pp. 298–299.

107 TO PETER GAST

Sils-Maria, 23 July 1885

Dear friend, I would have been willing to bet that you'd answer your despairing letter yourself in just the way to-day's card from you does — to my great delight, I'm happy to admit.[1] From my own experience in writing letters I'm only too familiar with the phenomenon I call "self-reply"; and I also know that it's both foolish and insensitive to interrupt this natural "recovery" (the restoring of one's personal sovereignty) with hasty declarations of sympathy. Listen to that! Spoken like a pedant — but felt like a friend, believe me. . . .

Yesterday, to fortify myself in my chosen way of life, I made a list of a number of traits by which I sense "refinement" or "nobility" in people — and what's "plebeian" in us. (In all my illnesses I have the horrible feeling of being pulled down to the level of plebeian weaknesses, plebeian softness, even plebeian virtues — can you understand that, healthy one?) It is noble, for instance, to have a resolute appearance of frivolity masking a stoic hardness and self-control. It is noble to go slow in all things, and to have a slow eye. We are not quick to admire. Precious things are few, and they come by themselves and seek us out. It is noble to shun petty tribute and to mistrust those who praise lightly. It is noble to doubt whether the heart can communicate; to regard solitude not as an option but a given. To be convinced that one has obligations only to one's equals and may deal with the rest as one sees fit. To have the constant sense of being someone with honors to bestow, seldom conceding that someone else might have any to dispense among the likes of us. To live almost always in disguise, to travel *incognito,* thus sparing oneself much indignity. To be capable of *leisure,* and not just the diligence of a chicken: cackling, laying an egg, cackling some more, and so forth. And so forth! . . .

---

[1] On 7 July Gast had written: "Blessed are those who don't submit operas. I can hardly work on anything; it all seems in vain and I haven't

the desire and energy to begin afresh. I won't be able to stand this much longer." The card, dated 21 July, says in part: "I've read a lot in *Zarathustra* lately and have derived strength from this peerless, holy book. If the real Zoroaster had written this book—oh my! . . . I've almost forgotten the opera business." (*BGN*, II, 32 and 34 respectively.)

108 TO FRANZ OVERBECK

[Sils-Maria, Summer 1886]

Dear friend, I too would very much have liked to see you again this year, but I know that it won't work out. My plan to spend the summer in the Thuringian woods and the fall in Munich is foundering on the *force majeure* (or *mineure*) of my illness. Life in present-day Germany is thoroughly unwholesome for me; its effect is poisoning and crippling. And whenever I'm there my contempt for mankind grows to dangerous proportions. . . .

So far Fritzsch has not been able to come to terms with Schmeitzner. But perhaps he will yet, since he seems to place great value on having "the entire Nietzsche" as well as the entire Wagner in his publishing house—a togetherness which thoroughly pleases me. For, everything considered, R. W. has so far been the only one, or at least the first, who's had some sense of what I'm up to. Thus Rohde, sad to say, appears not to have the foggiest notion, never mind any feeling of obligation toward me. In the atmosphere of our universities, even the best men degenerate. I am continually aware, even in people like Rohde, of a damnable universal indifference and a complete lack of belief in what they're doing. . . .

My discussions with all conceivable publishers have left me with but a single way out, which I'm about to take. I shall try to publish something at my own expense. If three hundred copies are sold, I'll get my money back and perhaps repeat the experiment. The firm of C. G. Naumann is lending its very distinguished name to the project. (This is confidential.) Schmeitzner's negligence is shocking: for ten years not a single copy sent to a retailer or a reviewer . . .

no advertisements whatever . . . a grand total of sixty-seventy copies of *Zarathustra* sold, etc., etc. Schmeitzner's excuse is always the same: for ten years none of my friends has had the courage to speak up for me. He wants 12,500 marks for my works. . . .

109 TO FRANZ OVERBECK

Sils-Maria, 5 August 1886

Dear friend, a bit of news and a request. Fritzsch just telegraphed from Leipzig: "Ours at last!" — words that make me very happy. So much for a disastrous blunder dating back to Basel days (a little too much trust, as so often in my life). . . .

The *new* book[1] . . . has just been finished; an order to send you a copy in Basel went out several days ago. Now the request, old friend: read it from cover to cover, and don't allow yourself to become embittered and estranged. Gather together all the resources of the good will you feel for me, your patient and so oft-tested good will. Even if the book as a whole is unbearable for you, some hundred particular details may not be. Perhaps it can throw a few rays of light on my *Zarathustra*, which is incomprehensible because it has its source in experiences unique to me.

If only I could give you some idea of my feeling of *isolation.* Neither among the living nor among the dead is there anyone with whom I feel any kinship. This is inexpressibly horrible; only the experience I've had, ever since I was a child, of living with this growing isolation makes it comprehensible why I haven't already been destroyed by it. Now the task for which I live lies clear before me, indescribably depressing — but transfigured by the consciousness that there's greatness in it, if greatness has ever made its home in the task of a mortal.

I'm staying here till the beginning of September.

[1] *Beyond Good and Evil.*

110 TO JACOB BURCKHARDT

Sils-Maria, 22 September 1886

Highly esteemed Professor, it pains me not to have seen and spoken to you in so long a time! With whom would I still want to speak, if I may no longer speak with you? The silence around me is becoming *too* powerful.

I hope that C. G. Naumann has done his duty by placing a copy of my recently published *Beyond Good and Evil* in your worthy hands. . . . I know no one who shares with me as many premises as you do. It seems to me that you've perceived the same problems and that you're working on them in similar ways — perhaps harder and more deeply, since you're more reserved. (But then I'm younger.) The uncanny preconditions of cultural growth, the extremely questionable relation between what's called "improvement" of mankind (or even "humanization") and the elevation of the species Man, above all the contradiction between every moral and every scientific view of life — enough, enough, here's a problem which, fortunately, I think, we seem to share with few among the living and the dead. Articulating it may well be the most dangerous venture there is, not for the one who dares to express it but for the one to whom it is addressed. My consolation is that for the time being there are no ears for my great new tidings — yours excepted, dear and honored sir, but then for you they will hardly be "new"!

111 TO MALWIDA VON MEYSENBUG

Sils-Maria, 24 September 1886

This is my last day here, dear friend. All the birds have flown. The fall sky is gloomy. It's getting cold. So "the hermit of Sils-Maria" has to be on his way.

. . . I've recently sent you a book. Its title is *Beyond Good and Evil: Prelude to a Philosophy of the Future.* (Forgive me! It isn't that you're supposed to read it, much less give me your opinion of it. People will *dare* read it, I suppose, some time around the year 2000.)

. . . In Germany it is always as if hostile winds were blowing at me, but I feel neither tempted nor obliged to blow back. It's simply the wrong environment for me. What concerns today's Germans is no concern of mine — which of course is hardly a reason to be cross with them.

Thus old Liszt, who knew how to live and die, nonetheless allowed himself to be entombed in the Wagnerian cause, the Wagnerian world — as if he unavoidably and inseparably belonged to it. That caused me much grief, for Cosima's sake. It is one more falsehood surrounding Wagner, one of those well-nigh insuperable misunderstandings in the soil of which his fame now grows and runs rank. Judging by the Wagnerians I've met so far, present-day Wagnerizing strikes me as an unconscious drift towards Rome, tending to do from within what Bismarck does from without.

Even my old friend Malwida — you don't really know her! — is in all her instincts profoundly Catholic, which by no means excludes indifference to dogmas and rules. Only a "church militant" needs intolerance; any faith deeply at peace and sure of itself has room for skepticism, for mildness towards other people and other things.

To conclude, I'll copy out a few words about me which can be found in the *Bund* (Sept. 16th and 17th). Title: "Nietzsche's Dangerous Book."[1]

"Those stacks of dynamite which were used in the construction of the Gotthard Pass had black warning flags, signifying mortal danger. In just the same sense, we speak of the philosopher Nietzsche's new book as a *dangerous* book. By so describing it we intend no more reproach for the author and his work than that black flag is meant to reproach that explosive. It is even farther from our thoughts, in alluding to the dangerousness of his book, to deliver this solitary thinker into the clutches of the ravens round the lectern and the crows at the altar. Spiritual, just like material, explosive can serve a very useful purpose; it need not be misused for criminal ends. Only one does well, wherever such stuff is stored, to declare plainly: 'This is dynamite!' "

So, dear friend, be very grateful to me for keeping a little distance from you! . . .

[1] The author was Joseph Viktor Widmann, a Swiss writer and editor of the *Berner Bund*. The review is by no means completely favorable: "To be sure, there is in all of these attacks an element of justified polemic, but much more of the close atmosphere of the study, too little of the sunshine of actual life." But as Gast comments, "This piece, taken as a whole, unquestionably belongs among the most intelligent things written in Nietzsche's lifetime about one of his later books." (*GBr* IV, 487.) Nietzsche and Widmann carried on a friendly correspondence in 1887 and 1888. Dynamite, by the way, had only recently been invented.

112 TO GOTTFRIED KELLER

Ruta Ligure, 14 October 1886

Highly esteemed Sir, honoring an old custom and an old affection, I've taken the liberty of sending you my latest book (at least my publisher Naumann was so instructed.) Perhaps this volume, whose content is a question mark, will run counter to your taste; perhaps its *form* won't. Whoever has applied himself to the German language earnestly and with genuine affection will simply have to do me a little justice: it is no mean task to give voice to problems as sphinxlike as mine.

Last spring I asked my aged mother to read me your *Sinngedicht*.[1] We both blessed you for it from the bottom of our hearts (and our throats, for we laughed a lot) — so pure, so fresh, so crystalline was the taste of this honey.

[1] Titlepiece of a short story collection (1881).

113 TO FRANZISKA NIETZSCHE

Nice, 22 December 1886

. . . My poor friend Gast had a terrible time in Munich and made no progress toward a performance. The whole affair touches me to the quick. Now he'll retreat to Venice again — but how disappointed, how embittered, how maltreated and humiliated! And this is a man who has created an *immortal* work! Well, I too went through this business, in that lovely year 1882. If you have what it takes, it doesn't kill you, and after all the story is as old as the world itself. . . .

114 TO FRANZ OVERBECK

[Nice, 9 January 1887]

My dear friend, a card to you left here just before your most welcome letter arrived. Hopefully your health will improve with the good care you have; man's solitude is never less of a blessing than when he has eye trouble.

The winter is hard, even here. Instead of snow we have rain for days on end; but for some time the nearby mountains have been *white* (which in this variegated and colorful landscape looks like coquetry on nature's part). This wealth of color includes, as usual, my blue fingers, as well as my black thoughts. With just such thoughts in mind, I'm currently reading Simplicius's commentary on Epictetus. It puts clearly in view the whole philosophical system which Christianity subscribed to, giving the work of this "pagan" philosopher the most Christian impact imaginable (granted the absence of the entire Christian emotive pattern and pathology: "love," as Paul speaks of it, "fear of God," etc.). The falsification of everything real by morality stands there in all its glory; a pitiful psychology; the philosopher reduced to a country parson. — And for all that *Plato* is to blame! He is still Europe's greatest misfortune.

115 TO PETER GAST

Nice [21 January 1887]

Dear friend, I'm genuinely relieved to know you're back in Venice. You can't imagine how your letter cheered me up. I felt as if it carried a promise that from now on things will go better for me as well — better meaning lighter, gayer, more southerly, more carefree, and hopefully less "literary." Making all these stage versions of my old writings has been painful, and has made me self-conscious. I'm not suited for redigesting my life. . . .

Recently I heard the prelude to *Parsifal* for the first time (in Monte Carlo, of all places). When I see you again I'll tell you about it in greater detail. But leaving aside all irrelevant questions (what purpose can or should such music serve?) and taking a purely esthetic point of view: Did Wagner ever do anything better? Here's the highest degree of psychological awareness regarding what's meant to be expressed, in the briefest and most direct form, with every nuance of feeling brought to the point of epigrammatic precision; a descriptive clarity reminding one of an embossed shield; and, finally, a sublime *coup* for which Wagner deserves the highest praise, a synthesis of things which many people (even "higher types") will deem incompatible: of austerity, of "elevation" in the frightening sense of the word, of insight and understanding which cut through your soul like a knife — and of compassion for what is seen there. You find the likes of this in Dante and nowhere else. Was there ever a painter who gave love so melancholy a face as Wagner does with the last accents of his prelude?

116 TO FRANZ OVERBECK

Nice, 23 February 1887

. . . By the way, those *Greeks* have a lot on their conscience. Falsifying was their true vocation. All European psychology suffers from Greek superficialities; and without that touch of Judaism, etc. etc. etc.

I read Renan's *Origines*[1] this winter, with much malice and little profit. This whole history of near-Eastern conditions and sentiments struck me as strangely abstract, lost in the clouds. My mistrust has reached the point of asking whether history is even *possible*. For what is it one wishes to determine? Something that in the moment of happening itself was indeterminate? . . .

I find this winter a refreshing interlude, a time for looking back. Incredible! In the last fifteen years I've launched an entire literature, and can finally, with the help of prefaces and additions, regard it as detached and liberated from me—and laugh, the way at bottom I laugh at all literary production. By and large I spent only my most miserable years doing it.

[1]*Histoire des origines du christianisme* (1863 ff.), of which the first and most famous volume is the *Life of Jesus.*

117 TO REINHARD VON SEYDLITZ

Nice, 24 February 1887

. . . During the last fifteen years Germany seems to me to have become a veritable school for stupefaction. Water, slush and bilge far and wide [-----]: that's how it looks from a distance. A thousand pardons if this offends your nobler sentiments, but for this present-day Germany, no matter how much it bristles like a hedgehog, I have lost all respect. It represents the stupidest, most degenerate, most untruthful form of the "German soul" ever,—and how much soullessness this "soul" has bitten off for itself! I forgive no one who compromises with it, even if his name is Richard Wagner, and especially not if it's done in the shamefully ambivalent and circumspect way this all too clever glorifier of "pure folly" permitted himself in his last years.

Here, in our land of sunshine, what different things concern us! Nice has just had its long international carnival (with a preponderance of Spanish girls, by the way); and close on its heels, six hours after the last girandola, there's been a new, much rarer attraction. The merry pranks of an earthquake (which has more than the dogs howling far and wide) have presented us with the interesting prospect of perishing. How delightful when these old houses rattle over your head like coffee-grinders! when the inkwell takes on a life of its own! when the streets fill up with terrified half-clothed figures, their nerves completely wrecked! Last night around two or three, jolly fellow that I am, I made a tour of inspection in the various parts of town, to find out where the terror was greatest. The people, you see, are camping in the open day and night; there's a downright military look about it. And the hotels! Quite a bit has caved in, so total panic reigns. I found all my friends strewn pitifully under green trees, all wrapped up because of the bitter cold, and responding to every little tremor with gloomy thoughts of death. . . . Apart from an old, very pious woman who is convinced that her God is not *permitted* to do her any harm, I was the only cheerful person amidst the ghostly faces and heavy hearts. . . .

118 TO PETER GAST

[Nice, 7 March 1887]

. . . It seems that Fritzsch isn't very enthusiastic about Part Five of *The Gay Science*. . . . Well, what publisher wouldn't be a bit fainthearted after having been naive enough to saddle himself with my writings? I haven't even managed to come up with any adversaries; for the past fifteen years not a single one of my books has received a serious, thorough, competent review. In short, Fritzsch deserves a little forbearance. . . .

A philologist has come here to see me who has an early history similar to my own, one Dr. A.,[1] a student of Rohde and von Gutschmidt, very highly regarded by his teachers, but—passionately sick of philology. He fled to me, "his Master," for he wants to dedicate himself body and soul to philosophy. So now I'm persuading him bit by bit not to do anything foolish and let himself be carried away by false models. I think I'm successfully disabusing him. . . .

Dostoevsky happened to me just as Stendhal did earlier, by sheer accident: a book casually flipped open in a shop, a name I'd never even heard before—and the sudden awareness that one has met with a brother.

So far I know very little about his career, his reputation, or his background. He died in 1881. In his youth he was in a bad way: illness, poverty (of the genteel sort), a death sentence at twenty-seven, a reprieve at the scaffold, then four years in Siberia, chained, among hardened criminals. This period was decisive. He discovered the power of his psychological intuition; what's more, his heart sweetened and deepened in the process. His book of recollections from these years, *La maison des morts,* is one of the most *human* books ever written. What I first read, just out in a French translation, is called *L'esprit souterrain,* and comprises two short novels:[2] the first a sort of strange music, the second a true stroke of psychological genius—a frightening and ferocious mockery of the Delphic "know thyself," but tossed off with such an effortless audacity and joy in his superior powers that I was thoroughly drunk with delight. Meanwhile I've also read *Humiliés et offensés* . . . with the highest respect for Dostoevsky the *artist.* And I've already noticed how the newest generation of Parisian novelists is completely tyrannized by D.'s influence and their envy of him (e.g. Paul Bourget).

I'm staying here until April 3rd, hopefully without further traffic with the earthquake. . . . Till now I've remained rather cold-blooded through it all, and have lived in the midst of crazed masses with a feeling of irony and cold curiosity. But one can't answer for oneself: maybe in a few days I'll be the most irrational person in town. The sudden and unexpected do have their charms.

And how are you doing? Oh, how your last letter buoyed me up! You are so brave!

[1] Heinrich Adams, who was half-American, half-Swabian.

[2] The first part of *L'esprit souterrain* is Dostoevsky's long story "The Landlady," while the second is *Notes from Underground.* The two parts are linked by a gratuitous invention of the French translators which turns Ordinov, the protagonist of "The Landlady," into the narrator of the *Notes.*

119   TO MALWIDA VON MEYSENBUG
[Chur, Switzerland, 12 May 1887]
. . . The solitude I've shared with nature has till now been my comfort, my means of recovery. Bustling, modern

cities like Nice and Zurich (from which I've just returned) end up making me irritable, sad, indecisive, despondent, unproductive, ill. . . .

The new (two-volume) version of *Human, All Too Human* is on my desk. . . . The long prefaces which I have found necessary for the new edition of my complete works tell with a ruthless honesty some curious things about myself. With these I'll ward off "the many" once and for all; people find nothing so infuriating as a hint of the constant severity one imposes on himself under the yoke of his own most personal ideal. I've thrown my hook out to "the few" instead, and even with them I'm prepared to be patient. For my ideas are so indescribably strange and dangerous that only much later (surely not before 1901) will anybody be ready for them.

To come to Versailles—oh, if only it were possible! For I greatly admire the group you associate with there (a strange confession for a German; but in present-day Europe I feel kinship only with French and Russian intellectuals, and not at all with my cultured compatriots who judge everything by the principle "Deutschland, Deutschland über alles"). But I must get back to the cold air of the Engadines. For me, spring is unbelievably oppressive; I hate to admit what abysses of dejection I fall into. My body (like my philosophy) takes to cold as though that were its natural element. This sounds paradoxical and unpleasant, but it's the most proven fact of my life. . . .

I too was notified by Frl. Salomé of her engagement, but I didn't answer her either, though I sincerely wish her prosperity and good fortune. This sort of person, so lacking in reverence, ought to be avoided. . . .

120 TO PETER GAST

Sils-Maria, 27 June 1887

. . . I cannot pass over in silence an event I'm having trouble coming to terms with—indeed, I'm still quite beside myself. Heinrich von Stein is dead. Very suddenly.

Heart attack. I was genuinely fond of him, and thought he'd be spared for my riper years. He was one of the very few people who made me happy by simply being there. He also had great faith in me. The last time I saw him he said that in my presence thoughts came to him he'd otherwise never have had the courage for; that I "liberated" him. And how we laughed together up here! . . . He was by far the finest specimen of humanity among the Wagnerians, at least so far as I've made their acquaintance. I'm so upset by this that I keep refusing to believe it. How lonely I feel! Sooner or later good old Malwida will die on me too — then how many will be left? I'm afraid to count. . . .

121 TO HIPPOLYTE TAINE

Sils-Maria, 4 July 1887

I've so many reasons to be thankful to you: for your kind and considerate letter, with its most gratifying reference to Jacob Burckhardt; for your incomparably powerful and clear portrait of Napoleon in the *Revue*[1] which I happened upon last May (I was somewhat prepared for it just then by M. Barbey d'Aurévilly's new book, whose concluding chapter, about new Napoleonic literature, sounded like a deep cry of longing — but for what? Surely for nothing less than your clarification and resolution of the enormous problem of monster and superman.). . . .

And now please allow me to present you with two of my books, which have just come out in new editions. I'm a hermit, as you shall see, and don't worry much about being read. Still, since my twenties (I'm forty-three now) I've never been without some excellent and devoted readers (always old men), among them Richard Wagner, the old Hegelian Bruno Bauer,[2] my esteemed colleague Jacob Burckhardt, and that Swiss whom I consider the only living *German* poet, Gottfried Keller. It would make me very happy to have the Frenchman I regard most highly among my readers too.

These two books are dear to my heart. The first, *The Dawn of Day,* I wrote in Genoa, during a period of the most painful illness, despaired of by my doctors, face to face with death, and in the midst of unbelievable privation and loneliness. But I wouldn't have had it otherwise, and was in spite of everything at peace with myself and confident. The other book, *The Gay Science,* I owe to the first rays of returning health. It came to being a year later (1882), also in Genoa, during a couple of sublimely clear and sunny weeks in January. The problems with which both books deal make one lonely. . . .

¹ *Revue des Deux Mondes,* Spring 1887.

² In his book *An Introduction to the Age of Bismarck,* Bauer had written of the nationalistic German historian and politician Heinrich von Treitschke: "Before he puts out a new edition of his writings we would recommend a study of the works of Friedrich Nietzsche. This German Montaigne, Pascal, and Diderot will afford him insights into history, into the character of peoples, and into the soul of ancient and modern literature which could lift him out of his confinement within his particularistic ecstasies." (Chemnitz, 1880, p. 287).

At the time, the pleasure Nietzsche derived from this tribute was small enough. To Gast on 20 March 1881: "To be sure, the author of *The Age of Bismarck* has called me "the German Montaigne, Pascal and Diderot." All at once! How little *discrimination* there is in such praise, hence how little praise!" (*GBr* IV, 54.)

122 TO META VON SALIS
[Sils-Maria, 14 September 1887]
. . . We're in the third and last stage of printing; the book will be called *Toward a Genealogy of Morals: A Polemic.* I've now provided a proper introduction to myself; the new prefaces, from *The Birth of Tragedy* to the *Genealogy,* constitute a sort of "developmental history". Nothing, by the way, is more disgusting than to have to comment on oneself; but since nobody else could possibly have taken the job off my hands, I clenched my teeth and did my best. . . .

123

TO PETER GAST

Nice, 10 November 1887

. . . The second volume of the *Journal des Goncourt* is just out, a most fascinating book. It covers the years 1862–65; in it the famous dinners *chez Magny* are described with great vividness — those dinners which brought together twice a month the most gifted and most skeptical Parisian minds of the age (Sainte-Beuve, Flaubert, Théophile Gautier, Taine, Renan, the Goncourts, Schérer, Gavarni, occasionally Turgenev, etc.). An exasperated pessimism, cynicism, nihilism, seasoned with a lot of exuberance and good humor; I wouldn't have fitted in badly myself. I know these gentlemen by heart, so thoroughly that I've had quite enough of them. You have to be more radical: at bottom they all lack the same thing — *la force*.

124

TO ERWIN ROHDE

Nice, 11 November 1887

Dear friend, perhaps I still need to make amends for last spring? As a token of good will I'm sending along to you a book that's just appeared.[1] . . . Don't become alienated from me so easily! At my age and in my state of isolation, I have no intention of losing the few people I once trusted.

Your N.

I beg you to come to your senses about M. Taine. The crude things you say and think about him exasperate me. I might forgive Prince Napoleon[2] for such an attitude, but not my friend Rohde. It's hard to believe that someone who misunderstands this type of austere and high-minded spirit (Taine is today the educator of all of France's more serious scientific minds) understands anything about my own task. Frankly, you've never said a word which allowed me to suppose that you knew of my destiny. Have I ever reproached you for it? Not even silently, if only because I'm not accustomed to hearing such a word from anyone else either. Who indeed could have responded to even an iota of the passion and pain that's mine? Has anyone had the faintest notion of the real cause of my long illness (which, however, I may now have mastered)? I've lived for forty-three years, and I'm still just as alone as I was in my childhood.

[1] *Toward a Genealogy of Morals.*
[2] Author of *Napoléon et ses détracteurs* (Paris, 1887), in which Taine is sharply criticized.

125 TO JACOB BURCKHARDT
Nice, 14 November 1887

My dear and most esteemed Professor, this fall once more I beg permission to set something of mine before you: a series of studies entitled *Toward a Genealogy of Morals* — and again, as always, not without a certain uneasiness. For (how well I know it) all the dishes I serve up contain so much that's difficult to digest that to invite guests, especially distinguished guests like you, to my table is really an abuse of friendship and hospitality. Such nutcracking should be performed alone, without risking anyone else's teeth. Psychological problems of the toughest kind are at stake, so that it almost takes greater courage to pose them than to venture solutions to them. Will you give me a hearing once more? I owe you these essays anyhow, since they are very closely linked to the book I sent last time (*Beyond Good and Evil*). Perhaps several key assumptions of that not very accessible work have come out more clearly here; at least I hope so. For everybody says the same thing about it, that they can't grasp what's going on, that it's some sort of "profound nonsense". — Two readers excepted: you yourself, highly esteemed Professor, and one of your most grateful admirers in France, M. Taine. Forgive me if I console myself now and then by saying: "I have had only two readers so far, but what readers!"...

In closing, I wish you good health. It looks as if this winter will be a severe one. Oh, if only you were *here*!!

126 TO GEORG BRANDES

Nice, 2 December 1887

... On my scale of experiences and events the rarer, the more distant, the finer registers predominate over the normal, middling ones. I also have (to speak like an old musician, which in fact I am) an ear for quarter-tones. Finally —and no doubt this above all is what makes my books obscure—I have a mistrust of dialectic, even of reasons. Whether a man is ready to call something true or not seems to me to be more a matter of the degree of his courage. (Only rarely do I have the courage to affirm what I actually know.)

Your expression "aristocratic radicalism" is very good. It is, if you'll allow me, the shrewdest thing I've seen about myself so far. . . .

Are you a musician? Just now a work of mine for chorus and orchestra, "Hymn to Life," is being published. Of my various musical compositions, this one is intended to survive and to be sung one day "in memory of me," assuming, of course, that enough of the rest of me survives. You see what posthumous thoughts occupy my mind. But a philosophy like mine is like a tomb—it seals one off from the living. *Bene vixit qui bene latuit:*[1] that's what's written on the gravestone of Descartes. An epitaph if there ever was one!

... I gave up my university professorship. I'm three-quarters blind.

[1] "Who has hidden himself well has lived well" (Horace).

127 TO CARL FUCHS

Nice, 14 December 1887

... Throughout the last years the vehemence of my inner vibrations has been frightening. Now that I have to move on to a new and higher form of expression, I need first of all a new sense of alienation, a still greater *depersonalization*. . . .

In Germany there's much complaining about my "eccentricities." But since it isn't known where my center is, it won't be easy to find out where and when I've thus far been "eccentric." That I was a philologist, for example, meant that I was *outside* my center (which fortunately does not mean that I was a poor philologist). Likewise, I now regard my having been a Wagnerian as eccentric. It was a highly dangerous experiment; now that I know it didn't ruin me, I also know what significance it had for me—it was the most severe test of my character. . . .

By the way, my understandably somewhat desperate publisher, the admirable E. W. Fritzsch in Leipzig, is ready to hand over a set of the new edition of my works to anyone who'll promise him in return a fair-sized essay giving an over-all view of me. The bigger literary journals like Lindau's *Nord und Süd* will shortly need such an essay, since there are signs of genuine alarm and agitation over the meaning of my writings. So far no one has had enough courage and intelligence to reveal me to my dear Germans. My problems are new, my psychological horizon frighteningly comprehensive, my language bold and clear; there may well be no books written in German which are richer in ideas and more independent than mine. . . .

128   TO CARL VON GERSDORFF

Nice, 20 December 1887

Dear friend, rarely in my life has a letter made me as happy as the one you wrote three weeks ago. I feel that our entire relationship has now been put in order again most thoroughly and honestly. Such a joy could not have been saved for a more suitable moment. My life has just now reached high noon: one door is closing, another opening. In the last few years all I did was settle accounts, balance the ledger; I've gradually come to terms with it all and have arrived at a fresh page. Who and what should still accompany me, now that I must move on (have been *condemned* to move on) to the real essentials of my existence, is a major problem. For, just between ourselves, the tension under which I live, the pressure of a great passion and a great project, is too enormous to allow anyone new to come near me now. The solitude around me is something frightful; all I can really stand any longer are total strangers, chance encounters—or those close to me from way back and from childhood. The others have crumbled away, or even been *thrust* away (much of it was painful and violent).

It was so moving to receive the gift of your letter, with its reaffirmation of an old friendship. Something similar happened last summer, when all of a sudden Deussen, whom I hadn't seen in fifteen years, turned up in the Engadine. (He's the first philosophy professor of Schopenhauerian persuasion, and maintains that I'm the cause of his conversion.) . . .

Just published, by E. W. Fritzsch: *Hymn to Life*. For full chorus and orchestra. Composed by Friedrich Nietzsche. Complete score. —Do please read the *new* edition of *The Gay Science*. It contains things which make one laugh.

129   TO REINHARD VON SEYDLITZ

Nice, 12 February 1888

Dear friend, if I've been speaking to almost no one it hasn't been a "proud silence," but on the contrary a very humble one, that of a sufferer ashamed to reveal how much he suffers. An animal crawls into its burrow when it is sick; so does *la bête philosophe.*[1] How rarely a friendly voice reaches me! I'm now alone, absurdly alone. And in the course of my relentless underground war against everything men have heretofore respected and loved (which I call a "revaluation of all values"), I myself have imperceptibly become something of a burrow, something hidden, which you no longer could find even if you were to go out to look for it. But of course no one does. Confidentially, it is not impossible that I am the foremost philosopher of this era, and perhaps even a little more, something decisive and ominous standing between two millennia. One is constantly made to pay for such a singular position—with an ever growing, ever more glacial, ever more piercing seclusion.

Our beloved Germans! Although I'm now in my forty-fifth year and have published some fifteen works (among them one *non plus ultra, Zarathustra*), they've not come up with a single half-decent review of even *one* of my books. They now resort to such expressions as "eccentric," "pathological," "psychologically disturbed." . . . And for years not a word of comfort, not a drop of human feeling, not a breath of love. . . .

[1] Nietzsche presumably means *la bête philosophique.*

130 TO GEORG BRANDES

Nice, 19 February 1888

Dear Sir, I'm most agreeably indebted to you for your contribution to the understanding of "modernity." Just this winter I myself am cruising in wide circles around this essential normative question, very high up, very like a bird, and with every intention of looking down on what's modern with the most unmodern eyes possible. . . .

On my next trip to Germany I plan to busy myself with the psychological problem of Kierkegaard. . . .[1]

I flatter myself that I've given the "new Germans" the richest, most deeply lived, and most independent books they own; moreover that I represent in my own person a crucial event in the crisis affecting all value judgments. But that could be a mistake, and stupid too. I would prefer not to *have* to believe anything about myself.

Just a few comments concerning my first fruits (the *juvenilia* and *Juvenalia*):[2]

My polemic against Strauss, the malicious chortling of a "very free spirit" at the expense of a man who thought he was one himself, caused a huge uproar. Though only twenty-seven then, I was already a full professor, hence a kind of authority, something *proven*. The most unbiased version of this affair (during which almost everyone who was anyone took sides for or against me, and a ridiculous amount of ink was spilled) can be found in Karl Hillebrand's *Zeiten, Völker und Menschen,* volume 2. Satirizing the senilities of an extraordinary critic was not what was at stake. Rather, I had caught the Germans red-handed in an act of self-compromising bad taste. In unison, despite sectarian differences, they had acclaimed Strauss' *Old and New Faith* as a masterpiece of freedom and subtle thought (even of style!). My essay was the first assault on German culture — the very "culture" which, we were told with such pride, had triumphed over France. The term "cultural philistine," my own coinage, survived this frenzied polemical exchange and has become part of our language.

Those two pieces about Schopenhauer and Richard Wagner, it seems to me now, are really a series of self-disclosures, and above all solemn commitments, rather than genuine psychological studies of these masters (as much my kin as they are my antagonists). I was the first to distill a sort of unity out of the two. Today this is a superstition very much in the forefront of German culture: all Wagnerians are disciples of Schopenhauer. It was different when I was young. At that time it was the last wave of Hegelians who supported Wagner. "Wagner and Hegel" was the rallying-cry in the fifties.

Between *Untimely Reflections* and *Human, All Too Human* there was a crisis and a sloughing of skin. A physical crisis too: for years I lived at death's door. This was my great good fortune — I forgot myself, I outlived myself. Later I brought this off a second time. . . .

[1] Brandes had written to Nietzsche on 11 January: "There is a Scandinavian writer whose works would interest you, if only they were translated: Søren Kierkegaard. He lived from 1813 to 1855 and is in my opinion one of the most profound psychologists of all time. A little book I wrote about him (translated and published in Leipzig in 1879) does not give an adequate idea of his genius, for this book is a kind of polemic, written in order to curb his influence. But from a psychological point of view it is probably the best I've published." (*G Br* III, 282–283.)

Nietzsche never did get to read Kierkegaard — or even, it would seem, Brandes' book about him. Considering the intensity of Nietzsche's responses to Luther, Pascal, and Dostoevsky, this is most unfortunate.

[2]Nietzsche means roughly: juvenile writings and Juvenalian satires.

131 TO PETER GAST

Nice, 26 February 1888

. . . What you say in your letter about Wagner reminds me of a remark of my own which I wrote somewhere: that his "dramatic style" is nothing more than a species of bad style, even nonstyle in music. But our musicians see it as progress. As a matter of fact, everything still remains unsaid — even, I suspect, virtually unthought — in this domain. Wagner himself, the man, the animal, the god and artist, infinitely surpasses the understanding and misunderstanding of our Germans. — And of the French as well?

Today I had the pleasure of being proved right in my answer to a question which may seem extraordinarily chancy: "Who was best prepared for Wagner? Whose nature was most deeply Wagnerian, though he had nothing to do with Wagner?" For a long time I'd thought it was that bizarre, three-fourths-mad poet *Baudelaire,* the author of *Les Fleurs du Mal,* regretting that this thoroughly kindred spirit hadn't discovered Wagner during his lifetime. I marked those passages in his poems which have a kind of Wagnerian sensibility, one to which no other poetry has given form. (Baudelaire is licentious, mystical, "satanic," but above all Wagnerian). — So what happens today? I'm thumbing through a just published collection of the posthumous works of this man whose genius the French deeply respect and whom they even love, and there, right in the middle of priceless specimens of the psychology of decadence (*Mon coeur mis à nu*[1] — the sort of stuff they *burned* in Schopenhauer and Byron), an unpublished letter from Wagner jumps out at me, referring to an essay of Baudelaire's in the *Revue européenne,* April 1861. Here's how it goes:

Mon cher Monsieur Baudelaire, j'étais plusieurs fois chez vous sans vous trouver. Vous croirez bien, combien je suis désireux de vous dire quelle immense satisfaction vous m'avez preparée par votre article qui m'honore et qui m'encourage plus que tout ce qu'on a jamais dit sur mon pauvre talent. Ne serait-il pas possible de vous dire bientôt, à haute voix, comment je m'ai senti enivré en lisant ces belles pages qui me racontaient—comme le fait le meilleur poème—les impressions que je me dois vanter d'avoir produites sur une organisation si supérieure que la vôtre? Soyez mille fois remercié de ce bienfait que vous m'avez procuré, et croyez-moi bien fier de vous pouvoir nommer ami. — A bientôt, n'est-ce pas?

Tout à vous, Richard Wagner[2]

(Wagner at that time was 48, Baudelaire 40; the letter is moving, albeit in miserable French.)

. . . During the last period of Baudelaire's life, when he was half insane and slowly going to pieces, they fed him Wagner's music as *medicine*; and at the mere mention of Wagner's name, "*il a souri d'allégresse.*"[3] (If I'm not completely deceived, Wagner wrote a letter of this sort, full of gratitude and even enthusiasm only one other time: after he received *The Birth of Tragedy*.) . . .

Of the many newspapers and journals to whom Fritzsch, in a very nice brochure last fall, offered review copies of my complete works, not a single one replied. . . .

[1] *My Heart Stripped Naked,* title of a collection of Baudelaire's aphorisms. The Schlechta text, p. 1280 (as well as *GBr* IV, 358) mistakenly has "*mon coeur mis à un.*"

[2] Dear Monsieur Baudelaire, I went to see you several times, but you weren't in. Of course you'll understand how much I want to tell you what enormous pleasure your essay has given me; no other words have ever honored or encouraged my feeble talent so much. Might it not soon be possible for me to tell you in person how intoxicating it was to read those beautiful pages which, like the greatest of poems, let me know what I cannot help boasting of—the impression I have made on a mind as distinguished as yours? A thousand thanks for what you have done for me, and please believe me when I say that I am very proud to be able to call you my friend. — — Shall I see you soon?

Yours devotedly,
Richard Wagner

[3] "He smiled with delight."

132 TO PETER GAST

Turin, 7 April 1888

... Dear friend, I'm availing myself of the first calm after a very stormy journey to write to you. Perhaps it'll bring me back a little peace and composure. For I've till now been coming apart at the seams, never before having traveled under such adverse conditions. How could anyone live through so many absurdities between Monday and Saturday? Everything went wrong, from the very beginning. For two days I lay ill—guess where? In *Sampierdarena*. Don't think for a moment that I wanted to go there. Only my trunk stuck to the original intention of going to Turin; the rest of us, namely my hand luggage and I, went off in various other directions. And what an expensive trip! How they preyed on my poverty! I'm really no longer fit for traveling alone; I get too excited, and do everything wrong. . . .

But *Turin*! My dear friend, congratulations! You've given me advice after my own heart. This is truly the city for me now. . . . Not at all a metropolis, not at all modern, as I'd feared; rather, a stately capital out of the seventeenth century, suffused with but a single dominant taste, that of nobility and the court. In everything an aristocratic serenity has been preserved. No shabby outskirts. A unity of taste right down to the very color (the whole city is yellow or reddish brown). . . . At night on the bridge over the Po—marvelous! Beyond good and evil!

The problem remains Turin's weather. So far it's made me exceptionally miserable. I can hardly recognize myself.

133 TO GEORG BRANDES

Turin, 10 April 1888

But what a surprise, dear Sir! What emboldened you to want to speak in public about one of the world's most obscure men? Surely you don't think I'm well known in my beloved fatherland? I'm treated there as if I were something singularly absurd, something one needn't for a moment take seriously. They seem to sense that I don't take them seriously either; and indeed how could I, at a time when "the spirit of Germany" has become a contradiction in terms? . . .

I've enclosed a small *vita,* my first. . . .

The Birth of Tragedy was written between the summer of 1870 and the winter of 1871 (finished in Lugano, where I was living with Field Marshal Moltke's family).

Untimely Reflections between 1872 and the summer of 1875 (there were to have been thirteen in all; fortunately my state of health said No!). What you say about "Schopenhauer as Educator" pleases me very much. This little piece serves as my identification card: he to whom it says nothing *personal* has very likely no other business with me either. It contains in essence the pattern according to which I've lived up to now; it is a stern resolve.

Human, All Too Human, including the two additions, the summer of 1876 to 1879. *The Dawn of Day,* 1880.[1] *The Gay Science,* January 1882. *Zarathustra,* 1883 to 1885 (each part took about ten days; I was absolutely "inspired." It was conceived entirely during vigorous hikes, with complete assurance, as if every sentence had been dictated to me. I wrote it with the greatest physical resilience and exuberance).

Beyond Good and Evil, summer of 1885 in the Upper Engadine and the winter following in Nice.

The Genealogy decided on, completed, and sent ready for printing to my Leipzig publisher, all between the tenth and thirtieth of July 1887. (Of course I did some philological things too. But they are no longer of any concern to either of us.) . . .

Vita. I was born October 15, 1844, on the battlefield of Lützen. The first name I heard was that of Gustávus Adolphus.[2] My ancestors were Polish nobility (Niëzky). The stock appears to have stood up well despite three German mothers. Abroad I usually pass for a Pole; just this last winter in Nice they had me down on the foreigners' list as Polish. I'm told that my head appears in Matejko's[3] paintings. My grandmother belonged to the Schiller-Goethe circle in Weimar; her brother became Herder's successor as ecclesiastical superintendent in Weimar. I was fortunate enough to be a pupil in the venerable Pforta school from which so many distinguished figures in German literature (Klopstock, Fichte, Schlegel, Ranke, etc., etc.) graduated. We had teachers who'd have brought (or did bring) honor to any university. I studied in Bonn, later in Leipzig; old Ritschl, then Germany's foremost philologist, singled me out almost from the first. At twenty-two I was a collaborator on the *Literarisches Zentralblatt* (Zarncke). The founding of the Philological Society in Leipzig, which still exists,[4] was my doing. In the winter of 1868–69 the University of Basel offered me a professorship; I didn't even have a doctorate at the time. The University of Leipzig thereupon gave me this degree, in a most flattering manner, without any examination, without even a dissertation. From Easter 1869 till 1879 I was in Basel; I had to give up my German citizenship, since as an officer (mounted artillery) I would have been called up too often and would have had my academic duties disrupted. I'm nonetheless expert with two weapons, saber and cannon—and possibly even a third. Everything went very well in Basel, despite my youth; on occasion, the examiner was younger than the candidate at doctoral examinations. I was very fortunate in that a cordial relationship developed between Jacob Burckhardt and myself, something quite uncommon for this aloof and hermitlike thinker. I had the even greater luck, right from the start of my life in Basel, to become indescribably intimate with Richard and Cosima Wagner. They were then living at their country place in Tribschen near Lucerne, cut off from all previous ties as though they were on an island. For several years our lives were as one, our trust in each other boundless. In Wagner's collected works, volume VII, there's a copy of an "open letter" sent to me on the occasion of *The Birth of Tragedy*. These connections gave me access to a large circle of interesting men (and women)—just about everyone between Paris and Petersburg. Around 1876 my health deteriorated. I then spent a winter in Sorrento with my old friend Baroness Meysenbug (*Memoirs of an Idealist*) and the congenial Dr. Rée. I didn't improve. An extremely persistent and agonizing pain in the head set in, exhausting all my energies. For several interminable years it got worse, reaching a peak of constantly recurring pain at which I had two hundred days of suffering a year. The malady must have had a purely localized source, there being no neurological foundation whatsoever for it. I have never had any symptoms of mental disorder, not even fever or fainting spells. My pulse at that time was as slow as the first Napoleon's (60). My specialty was resisting this extreme pain for two or three days at a stretch, remaining alert and fully lucid, though I was continuously spitting up mucus. There was a rumor going about that I was in a lunatic asylum (and had even died there). Nothing could be further from the truth. On the contrary, it was during this dreadful time that my mind first came to maturity. Witness *The Dawn of Day*, which I wrote in 1881, during a winter of unbelievable misery in Genoa, far from doctors, friends, and relatives. The book is a kind of "dynamometer" for me: I wrote it with a minimum of health and strength. From 1882 on things took a turn for the better, though very slowly. The crisis was overcome (my father died very young, at exactly the same age at which I myself stood closest to death). Even today I have to be extremely careful; I find certain climatic and atmospheric conditions indispensable. It's by necessity, not by choice, that I spend summers in the Upper Engadine, winters on the Riviera.

My illness has been my greatest boon: it unblocked me, it gave me the courage to be myself. . . . Am I a philosopher? Who cares?

---

[1] But see the *vita* below. (Nietzsche had more or less finished writing the book by November 1880.)

[2] King of Sweden, who fell on this battlefield in 1632.

[3] Jan Alois Matejko (1838–1893), well-known painter of scenes from Polish history.

[4] It continued in existence until after World War One.

Jacob Burckhardt, Hippolyte Taine, Georg Brandes,
Heinrich von Stein, Gottfried Keller, Friedrich Ritschl,
and Nietzsche

134 TO CARL FUCHS

Turin, 14 April 1888

Here too, just as in Nice, I have your picture on the table before me. No wonder I so often feel like talking with you—and do. Why, I ask myself, are we so absurdly cut off from one another by space (that space the philosophers say we ourselves have invented),—why this breach between the few people who have something to say to each other?

Have you ever been in Turin? This is a city after my own heart. In fact the only one. Serene, almost solemn. A classic place for foot and eye (because of superb pavements and a coloring of yellow and reddish brown that unifies everything). A fine touch of eighteenth century. Palaces to *our* taste, not Renaissance castles. And to see the snowy Alps from the center of the city, the streets seeming to run dead-straight into them! The air dry, sublimely clear. I'd never have believed that light could make a city so beautiful. Fifty paces from me there's the Palazzo Carignano (1670), my grandiose *vis-à-vis*. Another fifty and we have the Teatro Carignano, where they're doing a very creditable *Carmen*. . . . Everything here is open and spacious, especially the squares, so that in the middle of the city one has a proud sense of freedom.

It's here I've dragged my sackful of troubles and philosophy. The heat won't bother me till June. The proximity of the mountains furnishes a steady source of energy, even ruggedness. Then it's Sils-Maria's turn, my old summer residence: the Upper Engadine, *my* landscape, so far removed from life, so metaphysical. And then a month in Venice, a sacred place for me, since it's the home (prison, if you will) of the one man who makes music for me of the kind which seems impossible today: profound, sunny, loving, and in full freedom under law. . . .

135 TO GEORG BRANDES

Turin, 4 May 1888

... Today my "Hymn to Life"[1] will set out on its journey to Copenhagen. There's nothing we philosophers like better than to be mistaken for artists. ...

These past weeks in Turin, where I'll stay till the fifth of June, have been my best in years, especially for my philosophy. Almost every day for an hour or two I've mustered enough energy to look at my over-all conception from top to bottom, in such a way that the incredible variety of problems lies spread out beneath me in clear outline. This requires a degree of strength I'd almost given up hope of having. It all hangs together; for years now everything's been on the right track. You build a philosophy like a beaver: every move you make is indispensable and you don't know it. But this has to be seen, as I've seen it now, to be believed.

I feel so relaxed, so strong, so cheerful — I find myself pinning a donkey's tail on to the most serious things. ...

[1] In a letter to Nietzsche in April 1888, Brandes had asked for a copy of this composition.

136 TO REINHARD VON SEYDLITZ

Turin, 13 May 1888

... This time when I left Nice my black spirits left me as well. And, wonder of wonders, I've so far had a remarkably cheerful spring. The first in ten or fifteen years, maybe longer. ...

North winds, it seems, bring me good cheer. Just imagine, they are blowing my way from as far off as Denmark. For that's the latest news: at the University of Copenhagen Dr. Georg Brandes is currently giving a major series of lectures on the German philosopher Friedrich Nietzsche! According to the papers, they're going splendidly. The hall is always packed with more than three hundred people.

How long will it take for my *peripheral* effects (for I have followers in North America and even Italy) to react on my beloved fatherland? There, with a malicious solemnity, they've indulged me for years without so much as a murmur. That's very philosophical—and shrewd!

Yesterday I imagined a scene Diderot would have described as "maudlin morality." Winter landscape. An old carter, with an expression of the most brutal cynicism, harder even than the surrounding winter, is relieving himself against the side of his horse. The horse, poor abused creature, looks back gratefully, very gratefully. . . .

137 TO GEORG BRANDES

Turin, 23 May 1888

. . . By chance, a casual question today made me realize that one of life's most basic concepts has been blotted out of my consciousness: that of the "future." No desire, not the faintest trace of a desire do I feel. An empty slate! Is it because I've lived too long at death's door that I no longer open my eyes to all the lovely possibilities? What's certain is that I now confine myself to thinking from day to day, that I decide what shall happen tomorrow, and not one day further! Perhaps that's irrational, impractical, even unchristian—though yon mountain preacher did forbid concern "for the morrow"—but it strikes me as eminently philosophical. I respect myself just a little more for it. It seems I've unlearned how to desire, without even trying.

I've used these weeks to "revalue values." Do you understand this expression? When you come right down to it, the alchemist is the most praiseworthy of men: I mean the one who changes something negligible or contemptible into something of value, even gold. He alone enriches, the others merely exchange. My task is quite singular this time: I've asked myself what mankind has always hated, feared, and despised the most—and precisely out of this I've made my "gold."

If only I'm not accused of counterfeiting! Or rather, I'm bound to be. . . .

138 TO PETER GAST

Turin [31 May 1888]

. . . Dr. Brandes' lectures had a most happy ending – a big ovation, which Brandes insists was not meant for him. He assures me that I am now popular in all of Copenhagen's intellectual circles, and known in all of Scandinavia. It seems that my problems have been of considerable interest to these northerners; in some ways they were better prepared, e.g. for my theory of a "master morality," by their close acquaintance with the Icelandic sagas, which furnish the theory with excellent material. I'm pleased to hear that the Danish philologists approve and accept my derivation of *bonus*. Actually it was quite a coup to derive the concept "good" from the concept "warrior." Without my premises no philologist could ever have had such an idea. . . .

139 TO KARL KNORTZ[1]

Sils-Maria, 21 June 1888

. . . It is my deepest conviction that my problems, my whole "immoralist" position, come much too soon for this age, which is still far too unprepared for them. . . .

I believe my *Zarathustra* to be about the most profound work in the German language, and linguistically the most perfect. But to get a real feeling for this you'd first need whole generations experiencing for themselves the inner events that made this book possible. I'm tempted to advise you to begin with the last works, the most far-reaching and important (*Beyond Good and Evil* and *Genealogy of Morals*). I'm fondest of the middle period – *Dawn of Day* and *The Gay Science* (they're the most personal). . . .

I fancy that my books are first-rate with respect to their wealth of psychological insight, their fearlessness in the face of all that's most dangerous, and their lofty candor. Nor would I shun comparison regarding descriptive power and artistic form. I am linked to the German language by long-standing affection, genuine intimacy, and deep respect. Reason enough to stop reading nearly all books now being written in this language.

[1]Knortz (1841–1916) was born in the Rhineland, lived for some time in London, then emigrated to America in 1864. He spent four years as an instructor in Detroit, then was made Professor of German at Oshkosh College in Wisconsin. Thereafter he taught in Cincinnati and edited a German-language newspaper in Indianapolis. From 1886 on he devoted himself exclusively to literary and cultural-historical studies. Author and editor of several volumes of epigrams and poetry, Knortz received special recognition for his German translations of Longfellow and Whitman. He wrote several essays about Nietzsche.

140   TO FRANZ OVERBECK

Sils-Maria, 4 July 1888

. . . Since I left Turin I've been in miserable shape. Constant headaches, constant vomiting; all my old ills are back again, wrapped up in a nervous exhaustion which renders the entire machine useless. I'm having trouble warding off the most depressing thoughts. Clearheaded as I am, I have no choice but to be pessimistic about my condition as a whole. Not only health but its prerequisite is lacking: my vital energy is impaired. The ravages of ten years or more have taken their irreparable toll. All this time I've lived solely off my "capital" and put nothing, absolutely nothing back . . . . I am *not* suffering from a disease of the brain or of the stomach; but the pressure of nervous exhaustion— partly hereditary (from my father, who died solely of the aftereffects of a general lack of vitality), partly hard-earned —manifests itself in countless ways. . . .

141   TO FRANZ OVERBECK

Sils-Maria, 20 July 1888

Dear friend, nothing's improved, neither the weather nor my health—both remain absurd. But today I want to tell you about something even more absurd: Dr. Fuchs. He's written me *ad nauseam* (including a letter of twelve large, tightly packed pages!). It's gradually made me irritable, and brought back my old mistrust in full measure. His ego-

tism is so crafty and at the same time so ill at ease and con-
strained that all his talent and all that's genuinely artistic
in his nature is of no use to him. He complains that for seven
years in Danzig everyone was against him. . . . He held out
the prospect of an essay about my work, all the while in
mortal terror that standing up for an atheist like me would
damage his position as *organist* at St. Peter's. Naturally
he'd use a pseudonym! — he's already sworn both my publishers to secrecy. This same Fuchs also lived for years in
mortal terror that his friendship with me would get him in
trouble with Wagner; a few years before, when my influence in the Wagnerian world was uncontestable, he was
only too anxious to be helpful. I predicted that with Wagner's death he'd rediscover the courage to write me. And so
he has, in an almost comical fashion.

He's organist at the Synagogue in Danzig as well: you can
readily imagine how he makes fun of the Jewish service in
the filthiest way (but he accepts pay for it!!).

Finally he wrote me a letter about his origins, containing so many disgusting and gross indiscretions about his
mother and father that I lost patience and told him in the
bluntest way that I would not tolerate such letters. I am in
no mood to have my solitude disrupted by a flood of mail.
—So this is how matters stand. Unfortunately, I know this
type of person too well to entertain any hope that that's the
end of it. . . .

142 TO CARL FUCHS
Sils-Maria, 29 July 1888

Dear friend, I've asked that you be sent one of the few
copies of an unpublished work of mine — to indicate that all
is well between us once more and that the ferocious out-
burst of an all too vulnerable and all too solitary soul has
been successfully subdued. It's the fourth part of *Zarathustra,* which I've sheltered from the public eye with a modesty
I bitterly regret not having felt about the first three parts.
More accurately, it's an entr'acte between *Zarathustra* and

what comes after ("There are no names to describe you—"). . . .

If you should ever (but where are you to find the time, dear friend?) get around to writing something about me, do have the good sense, which alas no one else has had, to sketch, to "portray"—but not to "evaluate" me. . . . I've never actually had my portrait done, either as psychologist or as author ("poet" included). Nor as discoverer of a new kind of pessimism (Dionysian, born of strength, one that *enjoys* tackling the problem of human existence). Nor as immoralist (the highest form of intellectual integrity yet reached, *entitling* you to treat morality as illusion, once this integrity has become instinctive and ineluctable in its own right). It is by no means necessary, in fact not even desirable, that you take my side. On the contrary, I'd regard a good measure of curiosity, as if one were confronting a foreign growth with some ironical resistance, as an incomparably more intelligent attitude toward me. . . .

143   TO HANS VON BÜLOW

Sils-Maria, 10 August 1888

I have taken the liberty of encouraging a friend to send you the opening number of an opera. I thought perhaps it might whet your appetite. The opera is called *The Lion of Venice*. . . .

It is a bird of the rarest sort. They just don't write them like this any more. Here in bold relief are all the qualities which contemporary music (it's shocking but true) has lost. Beauty, the south, gaiety, a thoroughly good, even roguish mood in the very best taste, and the power to give a form to the totality of things without fragmentizing (a cautious euphemism for "wagnerizing").

My friend, Mr. Peter Gast, is one of the deepest and most gifted creatures whom fortune has flung into this impoverished era. My "pupil," I admit, in the strongest sense, a unique product of my philosophy. . . . He was a favorite student of old Richter[1] in Leipzig, and afterwards had a Wagnerian phase which he successfully surmounted. Since then he has been isolated in Venice, in admirably simple surroundings, unheralded, without cant, honors or other vanities. . . .

Now that Wagner dominates the opera houses from St. Petersburg to Montevideo, it requires a Bülowesque courage to risk *good* music.

[1] Ernst Friedrich Richter, Professor at the Conservatory and also Cantor at the famous Thomas School, a position formerly held by Bach. Edvard Grieg studied at this conservatory, founded by Mendelssohn and Schumann.

144 TO JACOB BURCKHARDT

[Sils-Maria, Autumn, 1888]

Highly esteemed Professor, I'm taking the liberty of placing before you a little piece about esthetics which, however much it was meant to afford relief from the seriousness of my tasks, has a seriousness of its own. Its light and ironical tone won't mislead you for a moment. I think I have a right to do some plain speaking about this "Wagner Case" — perhaps even a duty. The movement is now at the height of its glory. Three out of four musicians are wholly or partly converted; opera houses from St. Petersburg to Paris, from Bologna to Montevideo thrive on it, and the other day even the young German Emperor called the entire business something of the greatest national importance and placed himself at its head. Sufficient reasons to permit my entering the arena.

I realize that this essay, in light of the thoroughly European or international nature of the problem, should have been written not in German but in French. To a certain degree it was. It may in any case prove easier to translate into French than into German. . . .

(My address until mid-November will be *Torino poste restante*. A single word from you would make me happy.)

145 TO PAUL DEUSSEN

Sils-Maria, 14 September 1888

. . . This month you will receive a little polemic in the field of esthetics which, for the first time and in the most uncompromising way, reveals Wagner as a *psychological problem*. It's a declaration of unrelenting war against the entire movement. I alone, it appears, have enough scope and depth to be sure of myself here. The last report from my publisher indicates that something from me *contra* Wagner (a lampoon, if you insist) would cause quite a stir. So many orders poured in just on the basis of the advance notice that the edition of 1,000 can be considered sold (i.e., if the orders aren't cancelled later on). Read the essay from the viewpoint of style and taste as well: *no one in Germany today writes like this.* . . .

I already have another manuscript at the publisher's, a tart and crisp expression of my whole philosophical heresy— though hidden behind a good deal of charm and mischief. It is called *A Psychologist's Leisure*.[1] Both pieces are moments of relaxation from an immeasurably difficult and decisive task which, once understood, will split the history of mankind into two halves. Its meaning in four words: revaluation of all values. Much that has been subject to debate will no longer be an open question; thanks to decisions of the first importance concerning values, our reigning ideal of "tolerance" will be exposed as sheer cowardice and weakness of character. Being Christian, to name just one result, will from then on be *indecent*. . . .

[1] Gast suggested a more imposing title. Nietzsche, just then reading Bacon ("Four Great Errors" recalls Bacon's Four Idols) and doubtless having Wagner's *Götterdämmerung* (*Twilight of the Gods*) in mind, switched to *Götzendämmerung* (*Twilight of the Idols*).

146 TO PETER GAST

Turin, 14–15 October 1888

. . . Regarding *The Lion* Bülow never replied; but I paid him back. For this time it was I who wrote him a rude (and fully justified) letter, so as once and for all to be done with him. I let him know that "the foremost spirit of the age had expressed a *desire*"—I now allow myself the likes of this. . . .[1]

Turin is perfect, a splendid and singularly comforting place. It would seem impossible to find such stillness and solitude amid wonderfully broad and beautiful streets in the *best* part of a metropolis, right near the center. But this problem has been solved here. Quiet is still the rule, big-city bustle more or less the exception. This despite some 300,000 inhabitants. . . .

Just now, on the morning of the fifteenth, what do I find but your friendly birthday greeting. Heartfelt thanks—all the more since it's the only one! . . .

[1] To Gast, 30 October 1888: "Rude letters—in my case a sign of cheerfulness."

147 TO MALWIDA VON MEYSENBUG
Turin, 18 October 1888

Dear friend, these are matters in which I brook no contradiction. I am, regarding questions of *décadence,* the highest authority presently existing on earth. Our contemporaries, with their pitifully degenerated instincts, should consider themselves fortunate to have someone lighting up their darker corners for them. Wagner's knack for inspiring belief in himself as (you put it with such admirable innocence) the "ultimate expression of the creative temperament" did indeed require genius, but a genius for falsehood. I myself have the honor of being quite the opposite—a genius in the cause of truth.

148 TO FRANZ OVERBECK
Turin, 18 October 1888

Dear friend, yesterday, your letter in hand, I took my customary afternoon walk in the outskirts of Turin. Purest

October light everywhere; that wonderful tree-lined path — it led me along the banks of the Po for about an hour — hardly touched by fall. I'm the most grateful person in the world, *autumn*-minded in every good sense of the word. It's my great harvest time. Everything comes easy now, everything I do thrives, although I think hardly anyone has ever undertaken such momentous things. That the first volume of the *Revaluation of all Values*[1] is finished, ready for printing — I tell you this with a feeling I can't put into words. There'll be four books, appearing separately. This time, old artilleryman that I am, I'm moving in my big guns. I fear I'll be blasting the history of mankind into two halves. . . .

I'm moving against the Germans on all fronts; you'll have no cause to complain about "ambiguity." This irresponsible race, which has on its conscience all of our civilization's great disasters, and which at every decisive moment of history had "something else in mind" (— the Reformation at the time of the Renaissance;[2] Kantian philosophy just when a *scientific* way of thinking had been painfully achieved in England and France; "Wars of Liberation" on the advent of Napoleon, the only man who has ever been strong enough to forge Europe into a political and economic unity —) today has in mind "The Reich," this latest outbreak of separatism and cultural atomism at a moment when the great question of value is being posed for the first time. There has never been a more crucial moment in history — *but who'd be expected to know that*? The tension now arising is absolutely inevitable. At a time when mankind's most crucial problems are attacked with an unheard of freedom and intellectual passion which bid fair to settle their fate, this universal pettiness and apathy must be all the more blatant.

Toward me there is still no animosity at all. They simply don't hear anything I say, so they're neither "for" nor "against" me. . . .

[1] Nietzsche has in mind *The Antichrist,* but his frequently modified plans during these months cast doubt on the relationship of this work to a larger project.

149

TO GEORG BRANDES

Turin, 20 October 1888

Dear Sir, once again your letter brought a pleasant breeze from the North. You've so far been the only one to react favorably, indeed to react at all, to my attack on Wagner. For no one writes to me. I've given even my nearest and dearest a terrible scare. To name a few: my old friend Baron Seydlitz, unfortunately the current president of the Munich Wagner Society; my still older friend Councillor Krug of Cologne, president of the Wagner Society there; my brother-in-law Dr. Bernhard Förster in South America, that not unknown anti-Semite, one of the most zealous contributors to the *Bayreuther Blätter,*—and my esteemed friend Malwida von Meysenbug, the author of *Memoirs of an Idealist* who, as always, gets Wagner mixed up with Michelangelo. . . . Perhaps Bayreuth will defend itself in true German fashion by banning my books as "a menace to public morals." . . .

I too could tell some wondrous stories about the effect of *Tristan.*[1] A proper dose of spiritual torment strikes me as an excellent tonic to take before a Wagnerian meal. Judge Wiener of Leipzig tells me that the waters at Karlsbad would serve the same purpose.

You're so industrious—and I'm such an idiot, unable even to understand Danish! I quite agree that Russia is just the place for recuperation.[2] I count any Russian book, above all one by Dostoevsky (translated into French, for God's sake, not into German!!) among my greatest consolations.

[1]Brandes had written Nietzsche on 6 October: "At the risk of angering you, I must confess that *Tristan and Isolde* made an indelible impression on me. I once heard this opera in Berlin in a completely shattered, desperate state, and every note spoke to me. I don't know if the impression went so deep because I was so sick" (*G Br* III, 314).

150 TO PETER GAST

Turin, 30 October 1888

Dear friend, I just looked at myself in the mirror, and saw something totally new: a man in excellent spirits, well-nourished, and ten years younger than he has any right to look. . . . Days and days go by, all equally perfect, full of sunshine. Magnificent trees of glowing gold, the sky and the big river a pale blue, the air as pure as can be — a Claude Lorrain[1] beyond all my dreams. Fruit, grapes of the tawniest sweetness. And cheaper than in Venice! This is a good place to live in every way. . . .

The weather is so splendid that it's no great feat to do something well. On my birthday I started another project; it seems to be working out and is already quite far along. It's called *Ecce Homo, or How You Become What You Are,* and discusses, most audaciously, me and my writings. I wanted to introduce myself before embarking on the frighteningly solitary act of revaluation; I also want to find out just how much I can actually get away with under the German conception of a "free press." I suspect that the first volume of the *Revaluation* will be confiscated on the spot — quite legally, to be sure. *Ecce Homo* is designed to make the whole issue at once so serious and so fascinating that the commonplace and by no means unreasonable notion of what's *permissible* will just this once tolerate an exception. I speak about myself with all the psychological "cunning" and good humor possible; I have no wish to appear as a prophet or a moral monstrosity. Here too the book may do some good. Perhaps it will prevent my being mistaken for my very opposite. . . .

[1] A favorite of Dostoevsky's too, who had the opportunity to see some fine paintings by him during his four years in Dresden (1866–1870).

151 TO FRANZISKA NIETZSCHE

Turin, 3 November 1888

... We still abound in the finest grapes. A pound of the very best quality costs 24 *Pfennige* in German money. The food is unbelievably wholesome and good. It's not for nothing that I live in the most famous cattle-raising country, and in its royal seat at that. The tenderness of the veal is simply a revelation to me, as is the delicious lamb I love so much. And what cooking! What a sensible, simple, even subtle cuisine! I've never known until now what a good appetite can be. Honestly, I eat four times as much as in Nice, pay less, and haven't had a bit of indigestion. Granted that in this and other ways I'm singled out for special favors; I undoubtedly get the choicest morsels. But this is the case wherever I go—I'm taken for someone very distinguished. You'd be amazed with what pride and dignity your old offspring struts about here. ...

152 TO MALWIDA VON MEYSENBUG

Turin, 5 November 1888

Just wait a bit, most worthy friend! I'll prove to you yet that *"Nietzsche est toujours haïssable."* Without any doubt I've done you wrong; but as I'm suffering from a surfeit of righteousness this fall, it is a real treat for me to do wrong.

The "Immoralist"

153 TO FRANZ OVERBECK

Turin, 13 November 1888

... However much I try, old friend Overbeck, I can't find any bad news to tell you about myself. Things are proceeding in a *tempo fortissimo* of hard work and good spirits. ...

In the last few days we had the gloomy splendor of a state funeral in which all Italy took part: that of Count Robilant, the most admirable example of Piedmontese nobility (the natural son, by the way, of King Carlo Alberto, as is common knowledge around here). . . .

Meanwhile I'm getting rave reviews for my *Wagner Case.* Not only is it being hailed as a psychological masterpiece of the first order, in a domain no one had previously explored—the psychology of the musician—but they're saying that my analysis of the fundamentally decadent nature of German music is an event in the history of our culture which I alone could have brought off. . . .

Other good news as well. The most eminent Swedish writer, August Strindberg, whom Dr. Brandes calls a "real genius," has now spoken out in my favor. And St. Petersburg's high society is trying to establish relations with me, although greatly handicapped by the suppression of my works (Prince Urussov, Princess Anna Dimitrievna Ténichev). And last but not least, Bizet's charming widow!

The printing of *Twilight of the Idols, or How You Philosophize with a Hammer* is completed. The manuscript of *Ecce Homo, or How You Become What You Are* is already at the printer's. The latter, of the greatest importance, contains some psychological (even biographical) reflections about me and my writings; all of a sudden I'll be *visible.* The tone of the piece is gay and ominous, like everything I write. At the end of next year the first volume of the *Revaluation* will be out.[1] It's already finished.

[1] Nietzsche presumably means *The Antichrist* (see letter 148, note 1), which in fact was not published until 1895.

154 TO META VON SALIS

Turin, 14 November 1888

. . . That there is need for some enlightenment about me was recently made clear once again—this time thanks to Malwida. With a bit of an ulterior motive, I sent her a copy of the *Wagner Case,* asking her to look into the possibilities for a good French translation. "Declaration of war" against me: Malwida used those very words in reply.

Confidentially, I became convinced once more that this celebrated "idealism" is at bottom an extreme form of presumptuousness—"innocent," of course. She has always been allowed to have her say; it seems no one has ever told her that with every sentence she is not just mistaken, but *lying*. That's after all what "beautiful souls" do who can't bear to look reality in the face. Spoiled her life through, she ends up sitting on her sofa like a little comic oracle, saying: "You are quite mistaken about Wagner! I know better! He is another Michelangelo." So I wrote her that Zarathustra means to do away with the virtuous and the righteous, since they always lie. She answered that she agrees with me completely, for the *truly* virtuous are so few and far between! . . .

When I think of all I've perpetrated between the third of September and the fourth of November, I fear that the earth will begin to tremble again any minute. In Turin this time. Two years ago, when I was in Nice, it happened there, appropriately enough. As a matter of fact yesterday's observatory report did mention a slight tremor. . . .

155 TO GEORG BRANDES

Turin, 20 November 1888

. . . I've now told my own story with a cynicism that will become a part of world history. The book is called *Ecce Homo* and is a completely ruthless attack on the Crucified One. It ends with a stupefying burst of thunder and lightning against everything with the least taint of Christianity in it. I am the foremost psychologist of Christianity and, as an old artillery man, can mount heavy cannon which none of its opponents even dreamed existed. The whole thing is a prologue to the *Revaluation of All Values,* the work which lies finished before me. I promise you that within two years we'll have the whole world quaking. I am its undoing.

Can you guess who gets the worst of it in *Ecce Homo*? Our friends the Germans! I've told them terrible things. It is on their conscience, for example. that they robbed the

Renaissance, the last great period of western history, of its meaning. They did this at a moment when Christian values (the values of decadence) had succumbed, when even in the greatest Churchmen certain rival instincts, life instincts, had prevailed. To attack the Church, after all, meant trying to restore Christianity. (Cesare Borgia as Pope—this would have been the true meaning of the Renaissance, its proper symbol.)[1]

And you mustn't be angry to find yourself appearing in a decisive passage in the book[2] (I've just written it) where I condemn my German friends' behavior toward me, the way they leave me completely in the lurch, whether it's my reputation or the meaning of my philosophy that's at stake. You appear quite suddenly, enveloped in a nice little cloud of glory.

I believe every word you say about Dostoevsky;[3] and yet he has given me my most precious psychological material. I'm grateful to him in a very special way, much as he constantly offends my most basic instincts. It's rather like how I feel about Pascal, whom I almost love for the countless things he has taught me. He is the only logical Christian. . . .

[1] Cf. *The Antichrist,* section 61.

[2] *Ecce Homo,* "The Wagner Case," section 4.

[3] Brandes had written to Nietzsche on 16 November: "He is a great poet, but an abominable person, utterly Christian in his emotional life and at the same time utterly sadistic. All his morality is what you have christened slave morality" (*G Br* III, 319–320). In his letter of 23 November Brandes elaborated:

> Look at Dostoevsky's face: half a Russian peasant's, half a criminal's—flat nose, small, piercing eyes under lids that tremble with nervousness, a high, well-formed forehead, an expressive mouth that tells of endless torment, abysmal melancholy, unhealthy appetites, inexhaustible sympathy, passionate jealousy! . . .
>
> His heroes are not only the poor and the pitiable, but hypersensitive simpletons, noble prostitutes, talented, hallucination-ridden epileptics, rapturous seekers after martyrdom,—just the types we must assume to be rampant among the apostles and disciples of the early Christian era.

Surely there is no one further removed from the Renaissance.
(Ibid., pp. 325–326.)

156 TO AUGUST STRINDBERG

Turin, 7 December 1888

Very dear and esteemed Sir! Did a letter of mine go astray? I wrote you right after reading *The Father* for the second time, deeply moved by this masterpiece of strong-minded psychology. I expressed the conviction that your work is destined to be performed in Paris now in M. Antoine's *Théâtre Libre.* You ought flatly to demand this of Zola!

There's no question but that the hereditary criminal is decadent, even insane. But the history of criminal families, about which the Englishman Galton (*Hereditary Genius*) has collected the most impressive material, always leads one back to an individual too strong for his particular social environment. The latest major criminal case in Paris, Prado's, is a classic example. Prado was more than a match for his judges, even his lawyers, in self-control, wit, and bravado. This in spite of the fact that the pressure of the trial had already affected him so much physically that several witnesses recognized him only from old portraits.

But now a few words in confidence, in strictest confidence. When your letter reached me yesterday — the first time in my life a letter has reached me — I'd just finished the last revision of *Ecce Homo.* Since there is no longer any element of chance in my life, it follows that this is no coincidence either. How do you come to write letters that arrive at such moments?!

Ecce Homo should appear simultaneously in German, French, and English. Only yesterday I sent the manuscript to my printer. As soon as a page is ready, it is to go to the translators. But who are they to be? Frankly I had no idea that you had yourself rewritten your *Father* in such excellent French; I'd assumed that someone had skillfully translated it. If you should be willing to undertake the French translation *yourself,* I wouldn't know how to contain my joy over this miraculous and momentous good fortune. For, confidentially, translating my *Ecce Homo* requires a first-rate poet; in expression, in subtlety of feeling, it is a thousand miles beyond the capacity of all mere "translators." Still, it's not a big book. . . . Since it says utterly unheard of things and sometimes, in all innocence, with the voice of an emperor, we'll outsell even *Nana.*

Moreover, it is devastatingly and scathingly anti-German; it sides with French culture throughout (I treat German philosophers to a man as "unconscious counterfeiters"). Nor is the book boring — here and there I even wrote it in the style of a Prado. In order to safeguard myself against German brutalities (confiscation), I'll send advance copies to Prince Bismarck and the young Kaiser, and enclose a written declaration of war: military men cannot answer this sort of thing with measures appropriate to the police. I am, as you see, a psychologist.

Weigh it well, dear Sir! It is a matter of the greatest importance. For I am powerful enough to break the history of mankind in two.

There remains the problem of the English translation. Would you have someone to suggest for it? An anti-German book in England — —

157 TO PETER GAST

Turin, 9 December 1888

. . . Strindberg wrote to me for the first time the day before yesterday — I have never before received a letter that struck a world-historical note. He has grasped that *Zarathustra* is a *non plus ultra.* . . . Did I mention that Strindberg and Brandes are friends, that they both live in Copenhagen? Strindberg, by the way, thinks that I understand women better than anyone else in the world. *Ecco, Malwida!!!*

Yesterday I sent *Twilight of the Idols* to M. Taine, with a letter begging him to take an active interest in a French translation. I also have someone in mind for the English version: Miss Helen Zimmern, now living in Geneva where she is an intimate of my friends Mrs. Fynn and Miss Mansuroff. She too knows Georg Brandes (she brought Schopenhauer to England, so why not his polar opposite?)

I've made no progress with E. W. Fritzsch, but I still hope that if I am patient his price will come down a few thousand marks. If I can get all my works back for 8,000 marks, I'll have done well. Naumann is advising me in this matter.

Do pay a visit to my old friend Professor Paul Deussen as soon as possible (Berlin W., Kurfürstendamm 142). You can bring him up to date about what I am and what I can do. He is, indeed, very devoted to me, and in a way that's most rare in this world: last summer he sent 2,000 marks[1] for my printing expenses (and would you believe it, Frl. Meta von Salis sent 1,000 frs. for the same purpose!). This is confidential—please!

Now a very serious matter. Dear friend, I want all copies of *Zarathustra, IV* back, to protect it from mishaps (I read it in the last few days and almost died of emotion). It won't be ripe for publishing until after several decades of world-historical crises—*wars!* Please try hard to remember who has copies. According to my recollection: Lanzky, Widemann, Fuchs, Brandes, probably Overbeck.[2] Do you have Widemann's address? How many copies were there? How many do we still have? There may be a few in Naumburg.

The weather remains incomparable. Three crates of books from Nice have arrived. For several days I've been thumbing through my works, and for the first time I feel that I'm a match for them. Can you understand that? I've done it all very well, but never realized it before—on the contrary! For instance the various prefaces, and the fifth book of *La Gaya Scienza:* what a devil of a lot is in there! In *Ecce Homo* you'll discover something about the third and fourth *Untimely Reflections* that'll make your hair stand on end—it did mine. Both concern only myself, by way of anticipation. Psychologically speaking, neither Wagner nor Schopenhauer appears in them. I've understood the two pieces only for the last couple of weeks.[3]

Signs and wonders!

Greetings from the
Phoenix

—*Human, All Too Human* impressed me enormously. It has something of the serenity of a *Grand Seigneur*.

[1] According to Deussen (who may be being delicate), this was money he had been asked by an anonymous benefactor to transmit to Nietzsche. Schlechta (III, 1378) conjectures that Paul Rée may have been involved.

[2] And Gersdorff, who had been sent a copy in May of 1885 from Venice.

[3] But see Letter 130, to Brandes, 19 February 1888, second-to-last paragraph.

158   TO PETER GAST

Turin, 16 December 1888

. . . And now the most important thing. Yesterday I sent a manuscript to C. G. Naumann which will have to be done right away, i.e., before *Ecce Homo*. I can't find translators for *Ecce*; the printing will have to be delayed for several months. After all, there's no rush.

My latest will amuse you. You too appear in it—and how! It is called

Nietzsche Contra Wagner
A Psychologist's Portfolio

It is basically a study in antipodes, using a series of passages from my earlier writings in such a way as to provide *The Wagner Case* with a very serious companion piece. . . . Perhaps, by virtue of the curiosity *The Wagner Case* aroused, it will be widely read. And since I no longer write a single sentence in which I'm not fully discernible, this psychological counterpoint may well be the way to understand me—*la gran via*. . . .

159

TO CARL FUCHS
Turin, [18 December 1888]

Dear friend, it's all been going wonderfully. I've never experienced anything remotely like the time from the beginning of September till now. The most unheard-of tasks are child's play; my health, like the weather, shines forth each day with great brilliance and constancy. I can't begin to tell you what I've finished. *Everything is completed*!

In the coming years the world will be in utter turmoil. Since the old God has abdicated, *I* shall rule from now on.

My publisher has undoubtedly sent you *The Wagner Case* and, most recently, *Twilight of the Idols*. Might you be in a bit of a warlike mood? I would be most pleased if a — *the* — gifted musician would openly side with me now as an anti-Wagnerian and challenge the Bayreuth crowd. A small brochure telling all sorts of new and crucial things about me with particular emphasis on music — how does that strike you? Nothing lengthy; something sharp and rapier-like. It's a propitious moment. There is still time to disclose truths about me which may have become virtual inanities two years hence.

And what's with Danzig, or, I should say, *non*-Danzig?[1] Open up your heart again, dear friend — I have time, I have ears.

Warmest greetings from
the Monster

[1] Fuchs had frequently complained about the stultifying, even hostile environment that Danzig represented for him.

160

TO FRANZISKA NIETZSCHE
Turin, 21 December 1888

Dear old mother, in a few days, if I'm not completely deceived, it'll be Christmas. Hopefully my letter will reach you in time. . . .

The best news of all comes from my friend Gast, whose entire existence is miraculously transformed. Not only have Berlin's foremost artists, Joachim and de Ahna (the most demanding and fastidious breed to be found in Germany) expressed very great interest in his work, but you'll be even more amazed to learn that he moves only in Berlin's wealthiest and most fashionable society. His opera may have its first performance there — Count Hochberg is closely connected with these circles.

As a matter of fact, your poor old offspring is now a mighty famous man. Not especially in Germany, since the Germans are too stupid and vulgar for the grandeur of my genius and have always made themselves ridiculous where I am concerned, — but everywhere else. I have only the most select admirers, highly placed and influential people, in St. Petersburg, Paris, Stockholm, Vienna, New York. Oh, if you only knew with what words the foremost personages in the world express their devotion to me — the most charming women, not excepting one Madame la Princesse Ténichev. There are true geniuses among my admirers. No name is treated with as much distinction and reverence as mine today. . . .

161 TO FRANZ OVERBECK

Turin, Christmas 1888

Dear friend, we must settle the affair with Fritzsch quickly, for in two months I'll be the biggest name on earth.

I dare say things in Paraguay are as bad as they could be. The Germans they lured over there are furious, and are demanding their money back — which is all gone. There have been acts of violence. I fear the worst. . . .

What's remarkable here in Turin is the utter fascination I exert, though I'm the most unassuming person and ask for nothing. When I enter a large store the expression on everybody's face changes; on the sidewalk women stare at me.[1] My old street-vendor saves her sweetest grapes for me and has *lowered* her price! It was ridiculously low to begin

with. . . . My waiters are splendidly polite and coopera-
tive. . . . No one so far has taken me for a German. . . .

Nothing happens by chance any more either. Whenever
I think of someone, a letter from him arrives obligingly at
my door.

Naumann has a magnificent head of steam on. I suspect
that he kept the presses going over the holidays. Five gal-
leys came in the last two weeks. —*Ecce Homo* ends with a
dithyramb that's boundlessly expressive; I can't think of it
without sobbing.

Just between us, I'll be visiting Basel this coming spring.
I *have* to. It makes me damned mad never to be able to
speak freely to anyone. . . .

[1]Little wonder, if what Nietzsche mentioned to Gast a month earlier
had by now become habitual: "I play so many silly tricks on myself and
my head is so full of clownish private jokes that sometimes for a half hour,
in full view of everybody, I'll *smirk*—I can't think of a better word" (*G Br*
IV, 422). Cf. to Gast on 2 December: "Just got back from a great concert
. . . I was trying to recover from my extreme joy, and my face was continually grimacing—once, for ten whole minutes, tearfully" (*ibid.*, p. 423).
On 28 December Overbeck received a disturbing note. It read in part:
"I'm currently working on a memorandum for the courts of Europe concerning the formation of an Anti-German League. I intend to strap the
"Reich" into a straitjacket and provoke it into a war of desperation" (*BNO*,
pp. 452–453). Overbeck was reassured by a normal-sounding letter he received on 31 December. When Burckhardt brought him the note and letter of early January, 1889, Overbeck became really alarmed, sought professional counsel, and hastened to Turin.

162 TO CARL FUCHS

Turin, 27 December 1888

Everything considered, dear friend, from now on it no
longer makes sense to speak or write about me. With *Ecce
Homo,* the piece currently in press, I've settled the question of who I am once and for all. Henceforth no one should
be concerned with me, but only with the reasons why I am
here.

Nietzsche contra Wagner will appear first — in French too, if all goes well. . . . You mustn't take seriously what I say about Bizet. For someone like me, he is completely out of the question. But he provides a very effective ironic antithesis to Wagner. After all, it would have been incomparably tasteless on my part had I begun with, let us say, a eulogy of Beethoven. . . .

Don't neglect *Tristan*: it is a masterpiece and casts a spell which is unmatched not only in music but in all the arts.

I propose that you print Herr Gast's excellent essay about me as the introduction to your piece against Wagner. It would make a splendid impression:

The Nietzsche Case
by Peter Gast and Carl Fuchs

163 TO META VON SALIS

Turin, 29 December 1888

Dear Fräulein, will you allow me to send you a New Year's greeting? Hopefully it will be a good year. I don't want to say anything else about the one just ending — it was *too good*.

Meanwhile I'm beginning, in an utterly incredible way, to become famous. I doubt that any mortal has ever received letters of the sort I'm getting now — all from the elite of the intellectual world, whose characters have stood the test in high offices and positions. They come from everywhere, not least from the finest society in St. Petersburg. And the French! You should hear the tone of M. Taine's letters to me. Just now a charming, perhaps charmed message came from one of the leading and most influential men in France, who plans to concern himself with the publication and translation of my works — none other than the editor-in-chief of the *Journal des Débats* and the *Revue des Deux Mondes*, M. Bourdeau. . . .

Just so there's no lack of contrast: on my birthday my

sister wrote with the utmost scorn that I actually seem about to become "famous," and that it must be a prize collection of riff-raff which believes in the likes of me.[1] — This has been going on now for seven years!

And one more instance. I really do regard the Germans as a *rotten* species of mankind, and thank heaven that in all my instincts I'm a Pole and nothing else. When *The Wagner Case* appeared, my publisher, E. W. Fritzsch, allowed a most derisive article[2] about me to be printed in the *Musikalisches Wochenblatt,* which he himself edits. I wrote him at once: "How much do you want for my complete works? With sincere contempt, Nietzsche." The answer: 11,000 marks. You see? That's German!—the publisher of *Zarathustra!*

Georg Brandes is going to St. Petersburg again this winter, to lecture about that monster Nietzsche. He's really a most intelligent and good man. I've never had such exquisite letters. . . .

[1] Four days earlier Nietzsche, writing to Overbeck about his sister's birthday message, paraphrased her as saying that "I've certainly fallen in with some prize riff-raff, Jews who've licked in every pot, like Georg Brandes."

[2] By Richard Pohl; it was entitled "The Nietzsche Case."

164 TO PETER GAST

[Turin, 4 January 1889]

TO MY MAESTRO PIETRO

SING ME A NEW SONG: THE WORLD IS TRANSFIGURED AND ALL THE HEAVENS ARE JOYOUS.[1]

THE CRUCIFIED ONE

[1] Cf. Psalm 96.

165 TO GEORG BRANDES

[Turin, 4 January 1889]

To my friend Georg! After you discovered me, it was no great feat to find me. The problem now is how to lose me – –

The Crucified One

166 TO JACOB BURCKHARDT

[Turin, 4 January 1889]

My highly honored Jacob Burckhardt. That was the little joke on whose behalf I bear the tedium of having created a world. Now you are – thou art – our great, our greatest teacher. I, together with Ariadne, need only be the golden mean in all things, having in every respect such superiors – –

Dionysus

167 TO COSIMA WAGNER

[Turin, c. 4 January 1889]

Ariadne, I love you.

Dionysus[1]

[1] There were other mad notes – to Hans von Bülow, Malwida von Meysenbug, Overbeck, the King of Italy, the Vatican Secretary of State, the House of Baden, etc. The recurrent idea is Nietzsche's convocation of European potentates in Rome, with the Pope participating.

168 TO JACOB BURCKHARDT

[Turin, 5 January 1889]

Dear Professor, when it comes right down to it I'd much rather have been a Basel Professor than God; but I didn't dare be selfish enough to forgo the creation of the world. You see, one must make sacrifices, no matter how and where one lives. — But I did secure a small room, fit for a student, opposite the Palazzo Carignano (in which I was born as Victor Emmanuel), from whose desk I'm able to hear that splendid music coming from below me, in the Galleria Subalpina. I pay 25 frs. including service, make my own tea and do all my own shopping, suffer from torn boots,[1] and constantly thank heaven for the *old* world, whose inhabitants weren't simple and quiet enough.

Since I am doomed to entertain the next eternity with bad jokes, I'm busy writing, which leaves nothing to be desired, is very nice and not at all taxing. The post office is five steps away; I take the letters in myself, handing the great *feuilletoniste* over to high society. Naturally I'm on intimate terms with *Figaro*. And so that you'll have an idea of how harmless I can be, here are my first two bad jokes:

Don't take the case of Prado[2] too seriously. I am Prado, I'm also Prado's father, and I venture to say I'm Lesseps too. I wanted to give my Parisians, whom I love, a new concept—that of a decent criminal. I'm Chambige too—also a decent criminal.

Second joke. I salute the Immortals. Monsieur Daudet belongs to the Forty.[3]

Astu

What's unpleasant and a strain on my modesty is that in fact I am every historical personage; and as for the children I've brought into the world, I ponder with some misgiving the possibility that not everyone who enters the "kingdom of God" also comes *from* God. This fall, dressed as scantily as possible, I twice attended my funeral, the first time as Count Robilant (—no, he's my son, in so far as I'm Carlo Alberto[4] in my nature here below), but I was Antonelli[5] myself. Dear Professor, you really ought to see this edifice. Since I'm quite inexperienced in the things I'm creating, you have a right to make any criticism; I'll be grateful, but can't promise that I'll profit from it. We artists are incorrigible.

Today I looked at an operetta (ingeniously Moorish) and

took the occasion to ascertain, with joy, that now both Moscow and Rome are grandiose affairs. You see, my talent for landscape is undeniable as well. —Think it over; we'll have a really fine chat, Turin isn't far, no serious professional obligations tie us down, a glass of Veltliner could easily be procured. Informal dress is *de rigeur.*

With heartfelt love   Your

Nietzsche

I go everywhere in my student coat, now and then slap someone on the back, and say: *siamo contenti? son dio, ho fatto questa caricatura.*[6]

Tomorrow my son Umberto is coming here with lovely Margherita, but I'll receive her as well only in shirtsleeves.

The *rest* is for Frau Cosima — — Ariadne — —. From time to time we practice magic.

I've had Caiphas put in chains; I too was crucified last year in a long, drawn-out way by German doctors. Wilhelm Bismarck and all anti-Semites done away with!

You may make any use of this letter which will not lower me in the esteem of the people of Basel.

[1] Cf. Gottfried Benn's poem "Turin," in his *Gesammelte Gedichte* (Limes Verlag, Wiesbaden, 1956).

[2] Cf. Letter 156 to Strindberg, 7 December 1888, second paragraph.

[3] The Forty Immortals were the members of the French Academy. Daudet had just published in 1888 his biting satire of the Academy, *L'Immortel.* Its hero's name was Astier, which Bernoulli, II, 494 conjectures might have some bearing on the signature "Astu."

[4] Cf. Letter 153 to Overbeck, 13 November 1888, second paragraph.

[5] Papal secretary of state under Pius IX.

[6] "Is everything O.K.? I am God, this farce is *my* creation."

1844   15 October: Friedrich Wilhelm Nietzsche born in Röcken, Saxony, the first child of Pastor Karl Ludwig Nietzsche and his wife, Franziska.

1846   Birth of sister, Elisabeth.

1848   Birth of brother, Joseph.

1849   Death of father.

1850   Death of brother Joseph. Family resettled in Naumburg. Friendship with Krug begins.

1856   Much troubled by headaches and eyestrain.

1858   Obtains scholarship to Pforta School.

1859   Friendship with Deussen begins.

1861   Meets Gersdorff; composes music; is introduced to Wagner's *Tristan.*

1864   Graduates from Pforta with distinction in most subjects except mathematics. Two semesters at the University of Bonn, studying theology and philology.

1865   Abandons theology. Follows Professor Ritschl to University of Leipzig. Discovers Schopenhauer.

1866   January: first lecture to Philological Society. Friendship with Rohde begins. Enthusiastically pro-Prussian in war of 1866.

1867   October: begins military service. First philological essay published.

1868   Chest injury resulting from riding accident in March as member of cavalry troop. October: becomes Wagner enthusiast. November: first meeting with Wagner in Leipzig. On the staff of two journals, one philological, one literary. First portions of "On the Sources of Diogenes Laertius" published (the rest in 1869).

1869   February: appointed "Extraordinary Professor" of classical philology at University of Basel and instructor of Greek at the Pedagogical Institute. March: awarded doctorate by Leipzig. April: becomes Swiss national. May: first visit to Wagners in Tribschen, near Lucerne (also spends Christmas there). Summer: gets to know Burckhardt.

1870　Public lectures on "Greek Musical Drama" and "Socrates and Tragedy." April: made regular professor. Summer: writes "The Dionysian Conception of Life." August: obtains leave to serve as medical orderly in Franco-Prussian war. Early September: severely ill. Convalesces in Naumburg. Returns to Basel end of October. Friendship with Overbeck begins. Christmas in Tribschen again.

1871　Unsuccessfully bids for chair of philosophy at Basel. Health so bad by mid-February that he is relieved of duties for rest of winter semester. In Lugano with sister until early April, working on *Birth of Tragedy*.

1872　January: *Birth of Tragedy* appears; the Wagners are enthusiastic, Ritschl disappointed. April: considers giving up professorship for lecture tour in support of Wagner's new theater in Bayreuth. Wagners leave Tribschen for good. May: laying of foundation stone at Bayreuth. N. meets Malwida von Meysenbug. Wilamowitz' polemic against *Birth of Tragedy* appears; Rohde's reply published in October.

1873　N. works on *Philosophy in the Tragic Age of the Greeks* (published posthumously). Health more frequently poor. Gersdorff and Paul Rée attend N.'s lectures. The first of the *Untimely Reflections,* a polemic against David Strauss, is published.

1874　February: "The Use and Abuse of History," second of the *Untimely Reflections,* published. Summer: continued involvement with Bayreuth. Fall: enthusiastic response from Cosima Wagner to "Schopenhauer as Educator," published as third of the *Untimely Reflections.*

1875　Attacks of illness still more frequent and more

severe. Mid-August: moves into an apartment in Basel with sister. October: Heinrich Köselitz (Peter Gast), drawn to Basel by N.'s writings, begins attending N.'s and Overbeck's lectures.

1876 N. relieved of all lecturing duties by mid-February because of illness. April: proposes to Mathilde Trampedach. June: beginning of friendship with Gast. July: all four *Untimely Reflections,* including "Richard Wagner in Bayreuth," published in one volume. August: N. repelled by atmosphere at inauguration of Bayreuth Festspiele, flees to a forest retreat and begins work on *Human, All Too Human.* Returns reluctantly to Bayreuth for opening of *Rheingold;* makes friends there with Louise Ott and Reinhard von Seydlitz. October: health worse than ever; N. given full year's sick leave with pay. Travels with Rée to Sorrento to spend winter at Villa Rubinacci with him, Malwida, and his student Albert Brenner. Fall: last personal contact with Wagners. Continues work on *Human, All Too Human.* Reads Voltaire.

1877 Health deteriorates in Sorrento. Early May to end of August: taking cures in Switzerland (Ragaz and Rosenlauibad). After September 1: sharing apartment with sister and Peter Gast. December: partial reduction of teaching load once again for reasons of health. Break with Gersdorff.

1878 Beginning of January: Wagner sends *Parsifal* to Nietzsche. May: *Human, All Too Human,* I, published. August: Wagner attacks N. in *Bayreuther Blätter.* Fall: N. living alone on the outskirts of Basel, maintaining close personal contact only with Franz and Ida Overbeck.

1879 Health deteriorates to lowest ebb; treatment in Geneva at Easter ineffective. June: gives up professorship, is awarded a generous pension. First part of *Human, All Too Human,* II, published. Late June to mid-September: first lengthy stay in Upper

Engadine (St. Moritz). Poor winter in Naumburg, writing "The Wanderer and his Shadow" (concluding portion of *Human, All Too Human*). Reads Gogol, Twain, Poe.

1880   January: Rée visits N. in Naumburg. Mid-March to end of June: N. in Venice with Gast; dictates a sizeable portion of *Dawn of Day*. October: several weeks at Stresa, Lake Maggiore, very ill. November to April 1881: Genoa; finishes *Dawn of Day*.

1881   May and June: N. in Recoaro (near Vicenza); Gast visits all of May — N. is taken with his music. July through September: first stay in Sils-Maria. *Dawn of Day* appears. Reads Spinoza. October: returns to Genoa. November: discovers *Carmen;* begins work on *The Gay Science*. December: reconciliation with Gersdorff.

1882   January: N. working on Book IV, "Sanctus Januarius," of *The Gay Science*. Early February to mid-March: Rée visits N. in Genoa, then leaves for Rome, where he meets Lou Salomé. April: N. in Messina. Late April: meets Lou in Rome, then travels with her and Rée to Orta. Early May: in Basel with Overbeck. Mid-May: meets Rée and Lou in Lucerne; N. spends following month in Naumburg and Berlin. Late June to late August: Tautenburg (Thuringia); Lou and N.'s sister arrive together 7 August from Bayreuth. "Idylls of Messina" published. Quarrels with sister and mother over plans to live together with Lou and Rée in Vienna or Paris. End of August: N. sets Lou's "Hymn to Life" to music in Naumburg. Mid-September: breaks with mother and goes to Leipzig. Estrangement from Lou. Early October: N. has last meeting with Lou and Rée. Late November to late February: Rapallo.

1883   January: *Zarathustra,* I, written. Severe insomnia. 13 February: Wagner dies. Late February to beginning of May: Genoa. Then Rome, until mid-June; reconciliation with sister here. Summer in Sils-

Maria; *Zarathustra,* II, written in June and July. September in Naumburg; sister engaged to Bernhard Förster. Visits Overbecks early October on way south. October and November: Genoa. To Nice in December. *Zarathustra,* I and II, published.

1884 January and February in Nice: *Zarathustra,* III, completed. Late April to mid-June: in Venice with Gast, whose *Lion of Venice* he enjoys. Mid-June to early July: last stay in Basel; Overbecks see him through serious depression. Mid-July: visits Meta von Salis and others in Zurich; then to Sils-Maria. Brief, cordial visit with Stein late August. Fall: meets sister in Zurich; visits Gottfried Keller; has Gast's *Lion* overture performed for himself privately; November in Mentone. Early December to early April 1885: Nice, writes *Zarathustra,* IV; Paul Lanzky visits.

1885 February: arrangements for small private printing of *Zarathustra,* IV. 10 April to early June: with Gast in Venice; sister marries Förster, 22 May. Early June to mid-September: Sils-Maria, working sporadically on *Beyond Good and Evil.* In Naumburg until beginning of November. Then brief stays in Munich, Florence, and Genoa. Mid-November to beginning of May 1886: Nice.

1886 Mid-May to end of June: Naumburg and Leipzig (here last meeting with Rohde; several weeks with Gast). N. pays printing expenses of *Beyond Good and Evil.* Summer: Sils-Maria. Between August and October: writes prefaces to new editions of published works, and book five of *The Gay Science.* Travels in Italy in October, then settles in Nice again.

1887 January: discovers Dostoevsky. Spends April on Lake Maggiore. Then Zurich, seeing Overbeck and others. Mid-June to mid-September: Sils-Maria; Stein dies, 20 June; *Genealogy of Morals* written in July; Meta von Salis summer guest here; Deussen visits in September. Month in Venice with Gast. Late October: to Nice. November: end of friendship with Rohde; hears from Brandes.

1888   Early April: travels to Turin. News of Brandes' lectures on Nietzsche in Copenhagen. In Turin until early June, working on *The Wagner Case*. Then to Sils-Maria: *Twilight of the Idols* finished, *Antichrist* begun and finished in September. Returns to Turin later that month. October: breaks with Bülow and Malwida; writes *Ecce Homo*. November: in touch with Strindberg. December: *Nietzsche contra Wagner* prepared.

1889   January 3: N. collapses in Piazza Carlo Alberto. January 9: Overbeck brings N. to Basel. Within a week N.'s condition diagnosed as "progressive paralysis"; his mother arrives, takes him to Psychiatric Clinic at University of Jena. *Twilight of the Idols* published late January, and in spring *Nietzsche contra Wagner* (private printing). Early June: Förster takes his life in Paraguay. End of 1889: abortive attempts to cure N.

1890   Mid-May: mother takes N. home to Naumburg. Fall: sister returns from Paraguay, compaigns to save *Nueva Germania*.

1891   Spring: sister stops publication of *Zarathustra*, IV, allegedly fearing confiscation.

1892   Gast prepares new edition of N.'s complete works, including *Zarathustra*, IV. Sister returns to Paraguay beginning of June. N.'s mental condition steadily deteriorating.

1893   *Nueva Germania* collapses; sister liquidates her holdings and returns to Germany for good in September. October: Gast places N.'s literary estate in her hands.

1894   February: sister establishes a "Nietzsche Archive" in Naumburg family home, with musical soirées, etc.; stops Gast's edition of collected works. Personal break between her and Overbeck. Early summer: Gast relieved of all duties as collaborator on

Archive. Fall: Archive moved to more suitable quarters nearby. Fritz Koegel's edition of collected works begun (likewise not completed).

1895 *Antichrist* and *Nietzsche contra Wagner* published. September: Overbeck sees N. for last time; increased indications of crippling. December: mother yields to heavy pressure, signs legal ownership of N.'s literary estate over to her daughter.

1896 August: Archive moved to its permanent home, "Silberblick," in Weimar; N. moved there too.

1897 April: mother dies; her maid Alwine takes charge of N.

1899 A third edition of N.'s works begun.

1900 25 August: Nietzsche dies.

1901 Sister publishes a large number of fragments and notes from the 1880's as *The Will To Power,* volume XV of the latest edition of the collected works (rearranged and expanded into two volumes a decade later).

1908 *Ecce Homo* published.

Nietzsche's Major Works, with Dates of First Publication

Die Geburt der Tragödie aus dem Geiste der Musik (The Birth of Tragedy out of the Spirit of Music): 1872

Unzeitgemässe Betrachtungen (Untimely Reflections)

1. *David Strauss, der Bekenner und Schriftsteller* (David Strauss, Confessor and Author): 1873
2. *Vom Nutzen und Nachteil der Historie für das Leben* (On the Uses and Drawbacks of History for Life): 1874
3. *Schopenhauer als Erzieher* (S. as Educator): 1874
4. *Richard Wagner in Bayreuth* (R. W. in Bayreuth): 1876

Menschliches, Allzumenschliches (Human, All Too Human): 1878–1880

Morgenröte (The Dawn of Day): 1881

Die Fröhliche Wissenschaft (The Gay Science): 1882

Also Sprach Zarathustra (Thus Spoke Zarthustra): 1883–1885, 1892[1]

Jenseits von Gut und Böse (Beyond Good and Evil): 1886

Zur Genealogie der Moral (Toward a Genealogy of Morals): 1887

Der Fall Wagner (The Wagner Case): 1888

Götzendämmerung (Twilight of the Idols): 1889[2]

Nietzsche contra Wagner (Nietzsche contra Wagner): 1889,[3] 1895

Der Antichrist (The Antichrist): 1895

Ecce Homo (Ecce Homo): 1908,[4] 1911

All of these works were first translated into English in eighteen volumes under the general editorship of Oscar Levy (1909–1913). Most of them have been retranslated since, and are readily available in paperback editions. There is some variation in how the titles are translated (e.g. *Thoughts out of Season* = Untimely Reflections; *The Joyful Wisdom* = The Gay Science).

[1] Private printing of *Zarathustra*, IV: 1885; first public printing in 1892.
[2] The last four works listed here were all completed in 1888.
[3] Private printing.
[4] Limited edition.

The Correspondents

GEORG BRANDES (1842–1927)

The most eminent Scandinavian critic of his time, Brandes was raised in Copenhagen and trained for a career in journalism. But his scholarly and academic interests soon prevailed. He became a teacher and interpreter of literature, lectured at the University of Copenhagen, and finally, in 1902, was made professor. During a prolonged stay in Berlin (1877–1883), he broadened his contacts with distinguished artists and intellectuals, and made the acquaintance of some of Nietzsche's friends, including Paul Rée, Lou Salomé, and Heinrich von Stein. His critical principles as a literary historian were strongly influenced by Hippolyte Taine, whom he knew in Paris, as were his liberal political tendencies by John Stuart Mill.

A true cosmopolitan, he richly deserved Nietzsche's description: "good European and missionary of culture." His six-volume *Main Currents in Nineteenth Century Literature,* Darwinian in spirit, began appearing in 1871. He subsequently wrote separate works on Ferdinand Lasalle, Shakespeare, Goethe, Voltaire, Michelangelo, Disraeli, and Julius Caesar. His book on Nietzsche, in the main "An Essay on Aristocratic Radicalism," was published in English translation in 1914.

HANS VON BÜLOW (1830–1894)

Having studied the piano seriously from an early age, Bülow gave public performances during his teens in Stuttgart, became a Wagner enthusiast while working as a journalist in Berlin, and in 1850, following a performance of *Lohengrin* in Weimar, resolved to devote his life to music. He conducted at a theater in Zurich (where Wagner was at the time), then completed his piano studies with Liszt, whose daughter Cosima he married in 1857. Within a decade he had become royal pianist, conductor, and music director in Munich. He conducted the first performances of *Tristan* (1865) and *Meistersinger* (1868). It was in 1866 that Cosima left him for Wagner. He remarried in 1882, and was appointed director of the Berlin Philharmonic in 1887. A hard taskmaster, he became the model of a familiar genre of modern orchestral conductors: composers in their own right, who nonetheless see their primary mission as interpreting the works of others.

In July 1872, grateful for his inspired conducting of *Tristan* in Munich, Nietzsche sent Bülow a copy of his own symphonic meditation *Manfred* — eliciting an emphatic critical rejection. Ten years later, Bülow gave Peter Gast's work even shorter shrift. Nevertheless Nietzsche, in whose writings Bülow expressed periodic interest, remained on the whole well disposed toward this prickly, vibrant personality. An occasional dabbler in politics, Bülow was the most eminent German to sign Bernhard Förster's notorious anti-Semitic petition in 1880, and made a considerable stir in Berlin in 1892 when he rededicated Beethoven's *Eroica* to Bismarck.

JACOB BURCKHARDT (1818–1897)

Raised, like Nietzsche, in a vicar's house, Burckhardt belonged to a distinguished Basel family, many of whose members served in the local government or held positions at the University. He himself studied theology there for two years, then went to Berlin where he attended lectures by the great historian, Ranke. He spent an unforgettable summer in Bonn as an active member of its liveliest cultural group, Gottfried and Johanna Kinkel's *Maikäferbund* (he contributed some poetry to its magazine), returned for several semesters to Berlin, and spent the summer of 1843 doing research in Paris. Back in Basel, he completed his studies and worked as a political editor on the *Basler Zeitung*. Feeling at odds with the social and political upheavals that marked the rapid transition to "modernity" all around him, he quit his job in 1845 in order to rediscover and relive Goethe's classical Italy. Then in the fifties he produced his three greatest works: *The Time of Constantine the Great, The Cicerone* ("An Introduction to the Enjoyment of the Art Works of Italy"—something between a Baedecker and a cultural bible for Nietzsche and his friends when they toured Italy), and *The Civilization of the Renaissance in Italy.* By 1858 he had returned to Basel to devote himself fully to teaching.

When Nietzsche arrived in Basel, Burckhardt quickly recognized his extraordinary abilities. A general philosophical pessimism and a fondness for Schopenhauer afforded a common meeting ground, and Nietzsche was pleased that Burckhardt received his young friends, Gersdorff above all, with cordiality. Nietzsche had his students make a copy of Burckhardt's lectures on Greek cultural history (posthumously published with several references to Nietzsche's *Birth of Tragedy*); they formed the basis for one of the livelier "seminars" Nietzsche conducted with his friends in Sorrento during the winter of 1876–77.

Nevertheless, the much more isolated Nietzsche of the eighties made demands on Burckhardt for a critical and personal response which the older, more self-contained man was unwilling and perhaps unable to meet. Almost annually, Burckhardt was one of the first to receive a copy of a new work by Nietzsche. Each time the reply was polite and urbane, but reserved to the point of evasiveness. Finally, *The Wagner Case,* with its accompanying urgent appeal, received no reply at all. Clearly an element of "life-sustaining illusion"—it did not go unrecognized as such—played a role in Nietzsche's insistence on seeing in his beloved and admired Burckhardt a kindred spirit.

PAUL DEUSSEN   (1845–1919)

Nietzsche's friend from the time they were pupils together in Pforta, Deussen, in conformity with his heritage, made a brief but vain attempt at theology. He served as lecturer in philosophy in Berlin, and later became the first follower of Schopenhauer to receive a professorship. This was at Kiel in 1877, the year he published *The Elements of Metaphysics,* principally a survey of Schopenhauer's thought colored by his studies in Indian philosophy. In the first half of the 1880's Deussen belonged to the free-floating intellectual circle that included Brandes, Lou Salomé, Rée, Romundt, Stein, and the sociologist Ferdinand Tönnies. He made a reputation as editor and translator of Indian classics, and in 1911 founded the Schopenhauer Society. He published his *Recollections of Friedrich Nietzsche* in 1901.

ELISABETH FÖRSTER-NIETZSCHE (1846–1935)

Barely two years younger than Fritz, Lieschen (or Lisbeth) was as much Nietzsche's pupil as sister in their fatherless Naumburg home. The children were inseparable, and deeply happy together in their private world. Her idolization of him, his pleasure in her devotion and determination to be a good disciple persisted virtually throughout Nietzsche's Basel period. In May 1875, with Nietzsche's health in steady decline, his "Lama" came to Basel to keep house for him. This arrangement was maintained, with several interruptions, until the summer of 1878.

Two events highlighted a growing estrangement between brother and sister during the eighties: his encounter with Lou Salomé and her union with Bernhard Förster. Try as she might, Lama was unable to cope with the stormy advent of Lou in Nietzsche's life. Uneasy with the emancipated young intellectual from the beginning, she was further confused by her brother's inconsistent behavior. Not without his encouragement, she came to see the affair in a wholly negative light, and acted accordingly. The vindictiveness and moral self-righteousness with which she plotted to extricate her brother and rescue his honor came to be a mirror in which Nietzsche could see the ugliest aspects of his own complex character. Subsequently, his short-lived reconciliations with her alternated with attempts to lay much of the blame for his deep sense of frustration and loss at her door.

Förster's entry into Elisabeth's life was something of a crowning blow to Nietzsche. Born in 1843, Förster had joined the Wagnerian cause while a schoolteacher in Berlin. One of the leaders of Germany's anti-Semitic movement in the late seventies, he succeeded in organizing a mass petition with over a quarter of a million signatures (sent to Bismarck in 1881), demanding that Jewish immigration be curbed and that Jews be excluded from Germany's upper classes and educational posts. A prolific writer for the *Bayreuther Blätter,* the official organ of the Wagner cultists, he agitated in behalf of patriotism, racial purity, and vegetarianism. As an aftermath to a minor public brawl occasioned by one of his anti-Semitic outbursts, Förster was pressured out of his teaching position in 1882. Appalled by the degeneration of the Fatherland and inspired by the Wagnerian mystique to strive for the renewal of the German spirit abroad, he spent the next two years in Paraguay laying plans for *Nueva Germania.* He returned in 1885 to collect money, encourage settlers— and marry Elisabeth, who by this time was ready for a new commitment.

Her choice, from Nietzsche's point of view, could hardly have been worse. Though somewhat consoled by their being in far-off Paraguay, Nietzsche, the "good European" who had repudiated Bayreuth and all that it stood for, was dismayed that his loyal Lama had joined forces with such a man. Yet while he abhorred Förster's anti-Semitism and remained largely indifferent to the fate of the Paraguayan venture, he was not above expressing familial pride in its moments of glory as (false) reports from abroad reached him. The first bits of news about the actual situation in *Nueva Germania* came just prior to his collapse. The colonists, disillusioned by the well-meaning, idealistic Förster's incompetence and annoyed by Frau Förster's brave but high-handed efforts to compensate for her husband's inadequacies, began to rebel. In June 1889 Förster shot himself. Elisabeth tried to carry on, but the accumulation of mistakes and debts forced her to liquidate her holdings in the summer of 1893.

She quickly returned to her original cause. Establishing a "Nietzsche Archive" first in Naumburg and then in Weimar, she worked feverishly to make her brother a legend. Biographies were written, the collected works appeared in three different formats, archivists were hired and fired depending on the quality of their obedience to the whims of the directress, great quantities of new manuscripts and documents were made public—while others, putting her or her brother in an unfavorable light, were suppressed, destroyed, or "revised." The full dimensions of this scandal in German scholarship were not exposed until the mid-thirties. A highlight of the memorial services for Frau Förster-Nietzsche at the Archive in November 1935 was the presence of Adolf Hitler.

CARL FUCHS (1838–1922)

A one-time theology student, Fuchs was an early Schopenhauerian and Wagnerian. A gifted pianist and private pupil of Hans von Bülow, he eventually had a diversified career as musicologist, conductor, concert pianist, and (primarily in Danzig) music director, lecturer, and organist. His acquaintance with Nietzsche began in the early seventies, and before long his frequent, brochure-length letters had become legendary among Nietzsche's friends. He later made earnest efforts to gain public recognition for Peter Gast's music.

PETER GAST (1854–1918)

Born Heinrich Köselitz in Annaberg, Saxony, as the second son of a prominent family, he went to Leipzig in 1871 to study for a business diploma, but soon switched to musical composition. In 1874 he discovered *The Birth of Tragedy*

and the first two *Untimely Reflections,* and in the following
year moved to Basel to study under Nietzsche (and Overbeck, whom he had also read and admired). In the spring
of 1876 the by now fiery defendant of Schopenhauer and
Wagner offered to copy the manuscript of "Richard Wagner
in Bayreuth" for presentation on the latter's birthday. The
result was so impressive that from then on every manuscript by Nietzsche passed through Gast's hands, some to
be copied for the printer, all to be edited and proofread.
A warm friendship developed, and after Gast, a confirmed
bachelor, settled in Venice to write music in 1878, the relationship was maintained through correspondence and occasional visits until Nietzsche's breakdown. In an essay
written in 1888, Gast compared Nietzsche's appearance in
his life to that of Beatrice in Dante's *Vita Nuova.*

After 1889 Gast began an edition of Nietzsche's collected
works and wrote critical introductions to several of them;
the one to *Zarathustra* inaugurated a widely accepted view
of Nietzsche's development, interpreting it as having three
stages. In the wake of some rough treatment at the hands
of Nietzsche's sister when she returned from Paraguay, he
went home for seven years to write songs. But as the only
one able to cope with Nietzsche's at times almost inde-
cipherable scrawl, he was asked in 1900 to work in her
Archive, which he did until 1908. His willingness to col-
laborate on so questionable a venture as the Nietzsche
Archive, and to do so more or less on Elisabeth's terms, has
elicited surprise and criticism.

Of Gast's numerous compositions, only his comic opera
The Lion of Venice appeared in print (and then only as a
piano score). It had a single performance in 1891 under the
direction of Carl Fuchs.

CARL VON GERSDORFF   (1844–1904)

Born and raised in Jena, Gersdorff first met Nietzsche at
Pforta in 1861. The latter half of the sixties found him
studying law in somewhat desultory fashion in Göttingen,

Leipzig, and Berlin, reserving his militant enthusiasm for Schopenhauer, Bismarck's Prussia, and, for a time, vegetarian diets. After serving in the Franco-Prussian war, Gersdorff, who was very close to Nietzsche at this time, devoted himself to the Bayreuth cause, and then to a thorough study of land management in preparation for taking over his father's estate near Stuttgart. The estate occupied him for the rest of his life, although he spent much time reading, translating, and painting. In 1876 at Bayreuth he fell passionately in love with an Italian countess, Nerina Finochietti, whom he'd met earlier in Florence through Malwida von Meysenbug. The affair took on tragicomic proportions as it gradually implicated more and more of Nietzsche's and Gersdorff's mutual friends, dragged on interminably, had no satisfactory outcome, and left Gersdorff for a time embittered and alone. A candid, critical letter about this business from Nietzsche in December of 1877 ended their correspondence for four years. It was resumed by Gersdorff's announcement of his engagement to Martha Nitzsche (no relation), daughter of an old Lüneburger patrician family.

On visits to Basel during the early seventies, Gersdorff occasionally helped Nietzsche during his attacks of illness by taking dictation and correcting proofs. After 1876 the two never met again; but the reconciliation effected in 1881, largely through Peter Gast, who had comforted Gersdorff in Italy and had won his confidence, persisted until Nietzsche's collapse. Thereafter, Gersdorff maintained a friendly correspondence with Gast, Carl Fuchs, and Elisabeth Förster-Nietzsche. From his rural retreat, he gave the Archive moral support, though not without voicing occasional critical scruples, especially regarding the seven-year absence of Gast.

GOTTFRIED KELLER (1819–1890)

This famous Swiss poet, novelist, and short-story writer was born in Zurich. He studied landscape painting before turning to literature, and from 1861 to 1876 he served with distinction as state secretary of his native canton. Among his main works are the novel *Der grüne Heinrich* (1854–55; rewritten with a happy ending twenty-five years later), two series of short stories entitled *Die Leute von Seldwyla* (1856 and 1874), and another collection of stories, *Das Sinngedicht* (1881).

Nietzsche became a warm admirer of Keller's work in the early seventies. On the other hand, Keller's initial reaction to Nietzsche was sharply negative: he found the first of the *Untimely Reflections* (1873), directed against his friend David Strauss, puerile and in bad taste. Subsequently, Keller's attitude mellowed. Nietzsche began sending him copies of his latest works, and in 1884, at Keller's invitation, they met in Zurich.

MALWIDA VON MEYSENBUG   (1816–1903)

Descended from Huguenots, this daughter of a distinguished father and a highly cultivated mother enjoyed an exceptionally rich cultural upbringing in Kassel. The events of 1848 evoked in her strong populist and revolutionary sympathies, which lasted until late in life. They were strengthened by the experiences of the man she loved deeply at this time, Theodor Althaus, who spent three years in prison for his political activities and died in 1852. After a number of clashes Malwida finally emancipated herself from her family and went to Hamburg to teach in a girl's school. Here she met Carl Schurz, read with enthusiasm the writings of Wagner, and became an active supporter of the rights of women. She was forced to leave the country when her brother informed the authorities of her correspondence with various democrats living abroad. In exile in London and struggling to make ends meet, she was soon closely connected with Mazzini, Garibaldi, Gottfried and Johanna Kinkel, and the Russian revolutionary Alexander Herzen, whose memoirs she translated and whose motherless daughter Olga she adopted. Here she met Wagner for the first time.

While in Paris during the winter of 1859, she moved

freely in several popular salons, including Wagner's, and made the acquaintance of Michelet, Renan, Baudelaire, and Berlioz, among others. Thereafter she spent most of her time in Italy in search of a more agreeable climate. The work for which she is best known, *Memoirs of an Idealist,* received widespread critical acclaim when it finally appeared in German, almost a decade after the publication of the first volume in French in 1869. At the laying of the Bayreuth foundation stone in May 1872, Malwida met Nietzsche, and in the course of the following year most of his closer friends. There was serious talk of establishing a free university with people like Wagner, Burckhardt, Ritschl, and herself as guest teachers. Nothing came of the scheme, except perhaps one "winter semester" in 1876–77 when Malwida rented "Villa Rubinacci" in Sorrento to serve as a retreat for her, Nietzsche, Paul Rée, and Nietzsche's student Albert Brenner.

Later in 1877, Malwida settled permanently in Rome, leaving only for occasional visits to Paris and Versailles. Her circle of eminent acquaintances, including the race theorist Gobineau, was as rich as ever. In addition to her writing, she carried on in her many-sided role as mother and matchmaker to the younger generation of artists and intellectuals. The von Bülows became her closest friends, and when Hans von Bülow was chosen to direct the Berlin Philharmonic, this once passionate "Forty-eighter" consoled herself with the thought that he would be in the land of Bismarck.

ELISABETH NIETZSCHE.
See Elisabeth Förster-Nietzsche

FRANZISKA NIETZSCHE (1826–1897)

Nietzsche's mother, née Oehler, one of eleven children and rather minimally educated, married Karl Ludwig Nietzsche, pastor of Röcken, in 1843. Her natural high spirits and love of life were soon put to the test. In September 1848 her husband became seriously ill following an accidental fall, suffered miserably for nine months, and died at the age of thirty-six. He left behind Fritz (aged five), Lieschen (aged three), and the infant Joseph, who died suddenly not long after. The family moved to Naumburg, where the only adults in their home were Franziska, a grandmother, and two aunts.

The young, pretty, vigorous widow chose not to remarry, and placed all her hopes and expectations in her children. At an early age, Fritz's expressive intonations of biblical passages earned him the nickname "the little pastor." And the lonely, introverted, overly serious boy remained this for his mother even when he disappointed her by abandoning theology for classical studies. Impressed by the early promise of a distinguished career and sure of his love and devotion, Franziska was confident that her son's sternly moral, even ascetic mode of life would protect him from bad influences.

This confidence was severely shaken in the summer of 1882, when she learned of Nietzsche's plan to live in Paris with a young foreign adventuress. She shared Elisabeth's growing outrage over Lou Salomé and became convinced that she had a "lost son." The clashes that ensued brought out the worst in all three of them: Franziska blindly stood up for "Naumburger virtue," Elisabeth stopped at nothing to protect the family's reputation and keep alive her idealized image of her brother, who demonstrated how unready he was to live by the terms of his newly evolved philosophy. For the next two years Nietzsche's inner state was such that to Franziska his taking his life or losing his mind seemed very real possibilities.

When her son did collapse in January of 1889, Franziska feared that his books had provoked divine retribution. But she devoted herself wholly to his care, and read some false signs of recovery in the summer of 1890 as evidence of his return to God. At this time Elisabeth had difficulty persuading her, the legal owner of her son's literary remains, not to order his "godless writings" burned. Five years later she confided to Overbeck that her signing the legal rights over to her daughter had been, in effect, forced upon her. By now she had begun to take a critical view of Elisabeth's efforts on behalf of her brother's reputation—so much so that she considered writing a biography herself. Before her death in April of 1897 she had won the admiration of all who knew her for her selfless and skillful handling of her ever deteriorating son.

FRANZ OVERBECK (1837–1905)

Nietzsche's most trusted friend during his mature years, Overbeck had an unusually cosmopolitan background. He was born in St. Petersburg, the son of an Anglo-German businessman with a French wife. Relatives took charge of his early education in Paris, and he was resettled in Dresden at the age of twelve. By the time he had finished his formal studies in Leipzig in 1859, he was fluent in English, Russian, French, and German. Gradually committing himself to a career as an historical scholar, Overbeck remained in Leipzig until 1863, enjoying the close friendship of Heinrich von Treitschke. Then for six years he taught and studied in Jena, lecturing on the New Testament and early Church history, until a professorship in Basel, calling for him to teach precisely these subjects, was offered him in December of 1869.

Three months later he moved into an apartment below Nietzsche's, and by winter the two had begun to dine together daily in Overbeck's more spacious quarters. They kept this up for five years, sharing friends, enthusiasm for Bayreuth, and even the same publisher. Nietzsche's attack on David Strauss (actually on the state of German culture after the Franco-Prussian war) and Overbeck's polemic against the then fashionable theology (*Über die Christlichkeit unserer heutigen Theologie,* designed to show that true Christianity and modern culture are irreconcilable antitheses) went to press at the same time. But of course the differences between the two men were and remained marked. Overbeck became more and more of a scholar, and eventually the most consulted authority in his field, although he published relatively little, and most of this in a rather convoluted style.

When Overbeck married in 1876, his wife Ida soon became Nietzsche's confidante, as sympathetically concerned as her husband with his seemingly incessant physical tribulations and personal crises. For nearly two decades (from the time Nietzsche left Basel until his mother died in 1897), Franz Overbeck served as Nietzsche's unofficial business manager. The nearly two hundred exceptionally candid letters Nietzsche wrote to him after his departure from Basel indicate that for him Overbeck remained a discerning intellectual peer whose absolute integrity and independence of mind he admired and whose critical reservations he understood and accepted. Overbeck in his turn was to say of his friend, "Nietzsche is the man in whose company I breathed most freely."

It was Overbeck who hurried to Turin in early January 1889, confirmed that Nietzsche had had a mental collapse, took him to Basel for examination, saw him off to Jena to be committed and, together with Peter Gast, supervised Nietzsche's literary estate until Elisabeth took control in 1893. Dubious about her activities almost from the beginning, he refused to be enticed into the role of serving as a respectable front for the Archive. It was not until the end of his life that he released his letters from Nietzsche for publication, and then, stipulating that they be edited by independent hands, only to set a very distorted record straight.

Overbeck's final years were not happy. He looked with dismay upon the rise of yet another Christian theological establishment—one that availed itself freely of the historical and critical tools he himself had helped perfect. He left a number of his scholarly projects unpublished. A major one, *Christianity and Culture,* did appear posthumously (1919), as did a small series of autobiographical sketches (*Selbstbekenntnisse*) in 1941. Both Overbecks wrote valuable personal recollections of their experiences with Nietzsche.

PAUL RÉE (1849–1901)

In some ways the most remarkable but as yet the most obscure figure of importance in Nietzsche's life, Rée was born in Pomerania. In 1868 his family moved to Stibbe in West Prussia. Two years later he was wounded while serving as a volunteer in the Franco-Prussian War. He received his doctorate at Halle in 1875 for a dissertation in the history of moral philosophy which defended a number of skeptical theses. That same year he published *Psychological Observations,* a book of aphorisms, and two years later *The Origin of our Moral Sentiments.* His last work, *Philosophy,* published two years after his death, refers to his earlier writings as "unripe juvenilia" but retains in even more radical form their positivist-skeptical tenor.

After several futile attempts to establish himself academically, Rée began studying medicine in Berlin in 1885, finishing in Munich, and in 1890 settled down as village doctor in Stibbe. Here he lived a hermitlike existence, taking long hikes or working at his desk when time permitted. He frequently sent his poorer patients to clinics in Berlin and Breslau at his own expense, and brought them parcels of food and wine underneath his cloak. Decades later there were still villagers who remembered him as a holy man. In 1900 he left abruptly, moving to Celerina in the Upper Engadine to continue working as a doctor to the poor. On more than one occasion in his life prone to serious thoughts of suicide, he fell to his death on a mountain hike the year following and was ceremoniously buried by his grateful townspeople.

Rée first became acquainted with Nietzsche's circle of friends in the spring of 1873 in Basel, and this laconic young devoté of Schopenhauer impressed them as thoughtful, gifted, and utterly honest. By the following year, a warm friendship had developed between Rée and Nietz-

sche, who later invited him to share the Sorrentine retreat Malwida had arranged for his recuperation, beginning in October 1876. Nietzsche's friends alleged that he
was lured into his "positivistic" phase, his so-called
"Réealism" (roughly 1876–1882) by the younger man. It
seems likelier that seeds planted in Nietzsche by readings
of Friedrich Albert Lange and others much earlier had
now begun to germinate. The two friends' opinions of each
other's works were in fact largely negative—understandably so, since Rée had as little use for intuition and passion
in the realm of philosophy as Nietzsche had for long trains
of coldly logical thought from which the inner life of feeling
and desire had been ruthlessly severed.

In April 1882, following a lengthy visit in Genoa with
Nietzsche, for whom he had purchased an early (and not
very serviceable) model of a typewriter, Rée stopped off in
Rome. Here Malwida von Meysenbug, as fond of Rée the
person as she was repelled by his philosophy, introduced
him to her latest find, twenty-one-year-old Lou Salomé.
Rée and Lou at once became inseparable, and, after she had
turned down his offer of marriage, planned to live and
study together as "Platonic" brother and sister. They soon
invited Nietzsche to make it a threesome. Believing that he
had found in Lou his ideal soulmate and disciple, Nietzsche quickly agreed. But he may have had less Platonic
moments, for, according to Lou, he twice (the first time
through Rée) proposed marriage, only to be firmly refused.
A number of plans for living together were made and un-
made, either in deference to Nietzsche's fluctuating health
or because of opposition from Lou's family and Malwida.
By fall a dense cloud of misunderstandings, mutual suspi-
cions, and angry recriminations—for which Nietzsche and
his sister must bear the greatest burden of responsibility—
had poisoned the atmosphere. Although frequently ill and
periodically absorbed in *Zarathustra*, Nietzsche for many
months was the helpless victim of bitterness and rage,
himself given over to thoughts of suicide, or of challenging
Rée to a duel. He never saw either Rée or Lou again.

FRIEDRICH RITSCHL   (1806–1876)

This renowned classical philologist was born in a town not far from Erfurt in Thuringia. He studied in Leipzig and Halle, became professor at Breslau in 1834, spent a year doing research in Italy, then settled in Bonn in 1839. When Nietzsche arrived there in the winter semester of 1864–65 with the idea of studying both philology and theology, Ritschl was enmeshed in a well-publicized personal and administrative feud with his colleague, Otto Jahn. By the following fall, Ritschl had accepted an offer from Leipzig. Nietzsche, although privately siding with Jahn and not yet fully under Ritschl's pedagogical spell, followed him there, having resolved to concentrate on philology alone.

In Leipzig Ritschl's influence quickly predominated. He encouraged Nietzsche and the student friends who had transferred with him from Bonn to start a philological society, of which Nietzsche soon became president. He saw to it that Nietzsche's philological essays were published in scholarly journals, while his unusual candor gave the gifted pupil his first sharp insights into German professorial life. And when in December of 1868 he was consulted regarding a vacant chair of classical philology at the University of Basel, he recommended twenty-four-year-old Nietzsche, his doctoral work still uncompleted, so highly that the professorship was offered to him.

The warm personal friendship which Nietzsche had meanwhile developed with both Ritschl and his wife Sophie persisted until Nietzsche's annual visit to the family in 1873. On this occasion, the obvious divergence of their interests was exacerbated by a heated exchange about Nietzsche's commitment to Bayreuth. Two years of silence ensued, broken early in 1876 by a Nietzsche who had begun to work his way free of Wagner. Ritschl's reply gave promise of a renewed friendship, but the deteriorating health of both men interfered. Before the year was out Ritschl had succumbed.

ERWIN ROHDE (1845-1898)

The temperamental and sensitive child of a distinguished Hamburg physician, Rohde was sent to a private school in Jena where he excelled intellectually but remained introverted and isolated. Back in Hamburg to continue his studies, his multifaceted personality began to unfold. Having decided on a career as a classical philologist, Rohde began his advanced training at the University of Bonn in 1865, was attracted to Ritschl and, like Nietzsche, followed him to Leipzig. The two students, guiding spirits of the newly founded Philological Society, became exceptionally close friends. Nietzsche admired Rohde's facility with foreign languages, enjoyed his masterful mimicry of regional dialects, and felt kinship with the oscillations of his romantic sensibility, now surging with unbridled enthusiasm for Plato or Schopenhauer or Wagner, now ebbing into a bitterly ironic awareness of his own lack of creativity. Behind Rohde's crusty exterior there was a fragile, easily wounded ego; Nietzsche's sensitive affection and esteem were just what Rohde needed. They spent the summer of 1867 together—a time of relaxed comradeship neither was ever to know again.

In the winter of 1867-68 Rohde went to Kiel, where he studied, wrote, taught, and, in 1872, was made a professor. Meanwhile he had toured Italy and been taken by Nietzsche to see Wagner in Tribschen. When *The Birth of Tragedy* was attacked by Wilamowitz-Möllendorff, Rohde produced a vigorous polemic, dedicated to Richard Wagner, in rebuttal. In 1876 Rohde published his first major work, *The Greek Novel and its Predecessors,* and moved to the University of Jena. He married the following year and had three children.

Rohde's estrangement from Nietzsche began in 1878 with the appearance of *Human, All Too Human,* whose "Réealism" he found alien to Nietzsche's true nature (as did Malwida von Meysenbug). To Overbeck he expressed the conviction that Nietzsche would outgrow this, and that he would be better off if he stuck to classical scholarship. One of the very few in Nietzsche's circle who had a smooth-flowing, publicly successful career, Rohde came to frown upon his earlier polemical involvement on Nietzsche's behalf. A reunion in Leipzig in 1886 proved abortive, and because of Rohde's reticence Nietzsche never even met his family. A year later, Nietzsche's annoyance over Rohde's contemptuous dismissal of Hippolyte Taine occasioned the final break. When Rohde published his well-received *Psyche* in the 1890's, there was no mention of Nietzsche whatsoever, not even in a lengthy discussion of the orgiastic aspects of the Dionysian cult.

META VON SALIS-MARSCHLINS (1855–1929)

A self-reliant baroness, poet, doctor of philosophy, and writer on feminist questions, Meta von Salis had become acquainted with Nietzsche's family and friends several years before meeting him personally in July 1884 in Zurich. Nietzsche's last three summers in Sils-Maria provided opportunities for closer acquaintance. After 1889 she was for a time a sturdy friend and supporter of Nietzsche's sister, contributing the "Silberblick" house in Weimar where the Nietzsche Archive was to find its permanent home in 1897. That same year she published *Nietzsche: Philosopher and Nobleman*.

LOU SALOMÉ (1861–1937)

A general's daughter and native of St. Petersburg, Louise von Salomé fell in love at the age of seventeen with her tutor, Hendrik Gillot. Then in his early forties, a gifted preacher and a strong-willed, demanding person, Gillot instructed Lou in theology and philosophy. As a result of this training and her subsequent studies in Zurich, Lou proved to be the most knowledgeable of the three in modern philosophy when she, Nietzsche, and Paul Rée got together in 1882. From the very start Lou felt a deeper kinship with Rée, in whom she had complete confidence, than with the more complex and mercurial Nietzsche. Nevertheless, the many hours of uninhibited and intense conversation Lou and Nietzsche had together in Tautenburg remained unforgettable for them both.

There has been much conjecture about what, apart from outside interference, led to the estrangement between Lou and Nietzsche. Lou's autobiography (*Lebensrückblick*), written for the most part a half century later, offers two quite plausible reasons. One has to do with the side of Nietzsche which inclined toward the moral prophet, the mystic, the proclaimer of a new secular religion. This reawakened precisely those impulses in Lou which she had struggled to rid herself of. "Réealism" was what she really wanted; and indeed she did to some extent become Rée's disciple, although he was anything but the type to encourage it. The other reason likewise lay in Nietzsche. Lou suggests, and others corroborate, that Nietzsche found himself emotionally on something of an idealistic-sensual seesaw *vis-à-vis* the blue-eyed blonde with the classic Roman features. At any rate, Nietzsche's later insistence that he had always found her physically repulsive was far less sincere than were Lou's youthful efforts to keep her intimacies with men on a purely intellectual plane.

By the spring of 1884, Lou had overcome her chronic ill health, and in the year following she published under a pseudonym her first novel, *Im Kampf um Gott,* which impressed Nietzsche and his friends favorably. That winter, while Rée was studying medicine in Berlin, Lou met Friedrich Carl Andreas, at that time a German tutor. With Rée's blessing she married Andreas (who eventually became a distinguished professor of Middle-Eastern studies at Göttingen) in 1887. In later years she became a close friend of Rainer Maria Rilke, and trained in psychotherapy under Freud and Adler. A study which she published in 1894, one of the first serious efforts to deal critically with the phenomenon of Nietzsche, aroused heated controversy.

REINHARD VON SEYDLITZ-KURZBACH (1850–1931)

A student of law in Bonn and Berlin (his birthplace), Seydlitz was forced to abandon his studies because of ill health. After extensive travel his condition improved, permitting him to take up painting in Munich. He was one of the first to introduce the Japanese decorative style into Germany. His friendship with Nietzsche had its beginnings at the Bayreuth Festspiele in 1876. In the following year he and his bride shared Nietzsche's Sorrento idyll for several weeks. Liszt, Wagner, and Malwida von Meysenbug were also his friends. Seydlitz spent his later years writing and editing in the fields of art history and art theory.

HEINRICH VON STEIN (1857–1887)

Philosopher, esthetician, poet, and educator. While studying in Halle in 1874, he came to know Paul Rée and, subsequently, Malwida von Meysenbug, on whose recommendation he became young Siegfried Wagner's tutor. His pseudonymous first book (published at the age of twenty), *The Ideals of Materialism,* was well received. Nietzsche, himself impressed, did not meet Stein until 1882. Several memorable days together in Sils in the summer of 1884, during one of Nietzsche's periods of deepest isolation, gave promise of a close friendship and possible discipleship—a promise undermined by Stein's strong ties to Bayreuth and aborted by his sudden death at the age of thirty of a heart attack.

AUGUST STRINDBERG (1849–1912)

Studying the life of this great Swedish dramatist and novelist is an even more harrowing experience than reading his books or seeing his plays performed, for one is denied the comfort of telling himself that the self-lacerations he is witnessing are merely "fiction." Strindberg's writings are one long autobiography, and the painfully embarrassing and absurd events of his tortured existence seldom failed to find their way into print in barely disguised form. Strindberg's life has been called "an unending series of surgical experiments on his own brain and body." Nietzsche said much the same about himself, but Strindberg makes one aware that Nietzsche's sufferings might have been even greater: his loneliness was a burden, but it seems a relatively mild one when one thinks of two of Strindberg's marriages. And although Nietzsche was unhappy because not enough people took the shocking things he said seriously, he was at least, unlike Strindberg, spared a trial for blasphemy.

It was through Georg Brandes that Nietzsche and Strindberg learned of each other's existence in the fall of 1888. The congenial, animated correspondence that developed came to an abrupt end with Nietzsche's collapse. Strindberg is reported to have said later that Nietzsche alone had managed to put into words what he, Strindberg, had felt and thought.

HIPPOLYTE TAINE (1828–1893)

This distinguished French historian, critic, psychologist, and philosopher shared Nietzsche's ability to offend almost everyone by his writings, and, like him, lived in increasing solitude in his last years. He was of positivist persuasion, having rebelled against romanticism and what he called "spiritualistic" philosophy. For him, "no matter if the facts be physical or moral, they all have their causes; there is a cause for ambition, for courage, for truth, as there is for digestion, for muscular movement, for animal heat. Vice and virtue are products, like vitriol and sugar; and every complex phenomenon has its springs from other more simple phenomena on which it hangs." The causes of human behavior can be summed up under the headings of *la race, le milieu,* and *le moment.* The mental and the physical are "two translations of the same text."

Nietzsche sent Taine a copy of *Beyond Good and Evil*

in 1886, and a friendly though sporadic correspondence followed. Some of Taine's most important works are *La Philosophie de l'art* (1865), *De l'intelligence* (1870), and *Les Origines de la France contemporaine* (1875–94).

COSIMA WAGNER (1837–1930)

Born on Christmas day in Bellaggio on Lake Como, Cosima was the daughter of Franz Liszt and the French Countess Marie d'Agoult. This exceptionally gifted woman married Hans von Bülow in 1857, but had left him for Richard Wagner several years before Nietzsche first met her in Tribschen in 1869. To her organizational abilities, good sense, and tact belongs much of the credit for the Bayreuth Festspiele. She became artistic director after Wagner's death.

Nietzsche and Cosima were closest during his early years in Basel, when he visited Tribschen frequently. She left a lasting impression on him as the living embodiment of his ideal of womanly devotion and sensitivity. Moreover, she gave him considerable (though not altogether uncritical) encouragement during his period of gradual transition from philology to philosophy. Their final meeting took place during Nietzsche's stay in Sorrento in the winter of 1876–77. In *Ecce Homo* he paid her a lavish compliment: "The few instances of true culture I found in Germany were all of French origin, first and foremost Frau Cosima Wagner, by far the most outstanding voice I've heard in questions of taste."

To what extent the fantasy of playing Dionysus to her Ariadne (with Wagner in the role of Theseus) occupied Nietzsche's mind after his estrangement from his "Master" must remain a matter for speculation. Cosima's diary indicates that "Ariadne" received at least three love notes from "Dionysus" at the time of Nietzsche's breakdown. "My wife Cosima brought me here," Nietzsche told his doctors at the psychiatric clinic in Jena late in March, 1889.

RICHARD WAGNER (1813-1883)

Wagner's tempestuous career, with its recurrent financial, political and amatory crises, cannot be summarized briefly — nor is any detailed knowledge of it necessary for our purposes. The reader who is interested in him would do well to consult Ernest Newman's excellent four-volume biography; of particular relevance is volume four, which contains a great many pages, some of them highly critical, devoted to Nietzsche.

Richard Wagner was a supremely egotistical man who wanted not collaborators but adoring disciples around him. And soon after Nietzsche first met Wagner early in 1869, he did become the older man's disciple. But it was only to be expected that the maturing Nietzsche would eventually feel the need for a declaration of independence. Perhaps too, Wagner's tendency to classify people as either great admirers or great enemies was catching. At any rate, as Nietzsche's own ego grew in the unhappy soil of his increasing isolation, he found it necessary to reject his former idol. There were, indeed, many good reasons for complaining about Wagner and his cult. And some of Nietzsche's trenchant analyses of Wagner's operas have never been surpassed.

Bibliography / Index

Bibliography

PART ONE: SOURCES FOR THE CORRESPONDENCE

Three general collections of Nietzsche's letters are indispensable. They are:

(1) *Friedrich Nietzsches Gesammelte Briefe,* 5 volumes. Their content is as follows. *Volume One,* third edition, edited by Elisabeth Förster-Nietzsche and Peter Gast. Berlin and Leipzig: Schuster and Loeffler, 1902. Letters to Marie Baumgartner, Deussen, Fuchs, Gersdorff, Krug, Louise Ott, Seydlitz, and others. There are some 30 fewer letters in the first two editions, whose format differs as well. *Volume Two,* second edition, edited by Elisabeth Förster-Nietzsche and Fritz Schöll. Berlin and Leipzig: Schuster and Loeffler, 1902. Letters to and from Rohde. Reissued without changes in 1923. *Volume Three,* second edition, edited by Elisabeth Förster-Nietzsche, Curt Wachsmuth, and Peter Gast. Leipzig: Insel, 1905. Letters to Brandes, Bülow, Burckhardt, Keller, Meysenbug, Ritschl, Senger, Stein, and Taine. A slightly modified edition appeared in 1919. *Volume Four,* edited by Peter Gast. Insel, 1908. Letters to Gast. *Volume Five* (two separate parts), edited by Elisabeth Förster-Nietzsche, Insel, 1909. Letters to mother and sister; part two contains a few letters and drafts of letters to others as well, notably Förster, Rée, and Lou Salomé (a revised edition in 1926 omits these). Users of this volume should consult Schlechta, III (below) pp. 1371–1378, 1408–1423. (2) *Friedrich Nietzsche: Historisch-Kritische Gesamtausgabe der Briefe,* 4 volumes. Edited by Wilhelm Hoppe and Karl Schlechta. Munich: C. H. Beck, 1938–1942. The war interrupted their work when they had reached early May 1877; no further volumes have been published. There is an extensive report on the sources of the letters at the beginning of vol. I. At that time, some 2,400 original letters by Nietzsche were known to Schlechta and Hoppe; some 1,700 were in the possession of the Archive, including almost 800 to relatives.

(3) *Friedrich Nietzsche: Werke in drei Bänden.* Edited by Karl Schlechta. Munich: Carl Hanser, 1966. Vol. III has 278 letters, a very thorough chronology, and a critical report concerning the authenticity of some of the letters by Nietzsche that were published under Elisabeth Förster-Nietzsche's supervision.

In addition, three ample selections of Nietzsche's letters are of interest because they were edited with considerable supporting scholarship: *Nietzsche in seinen Briefen.* Edited by Alfred Baeumler. Leipzig: Alfred Kröner, 1932. *La Vie de Frédéric Nietzsche d 'après sa Correspondance.* Edited and translated by Georges Walz. Paris: Rieder, 1932. *Selected Letters of Friedrich Nietzsche.* Edited and translated by Christopher Middleton. Chicago: University of Chicago Press, 1969.

The following more specialized collections are particularly helpful:

Die Briefe Peter Gasts an Friedrich Nietzsche. 2 vols. Edited by A. Mendt. Munich: Nietzsche-Gesellschaft, 1923 and 1924.
Die Briefe des Freiherrn Carl von Gersdorff an F. N., 3 vols. Edited by Karl Schlechta. Weimar: Gesellschaft der Freunde des Nietzsche-Archivs, 1934–1936. A supplementary volume, edited by Erhart Thierbach in 1937, has a selection of Gersdorff's letters concerning Nietzsche to Elisabeth Förster-Nietzsche, Fuchs, Gast, Rohde, and the Wagners. It also has a thorough index for all four volumes.
Briefe von und an Malwida von Meysenbug. Edited by Berta Schleicher. Berlin: Schuster and Loeffler, 1920.
Der kranke Nietzsche. (His mother's letters to Franz Overbeck from 1889 to 1897), edited by Erich Podach. Vienna: Bermann-Fischer, 1937.
Nietzsches Briefwechsel mit Franz Overbeck. Edited by Richard Oehler and Carl Albrecht Bernoulli. Leipzig: Insel, 1916.

Nietzsche und Strindberg. Mit ihrem Briefwechsel. Karl
Strecker, Munich: Georg Müller, 1921.
Die Briefe Cosima Wagners an Friedrich Nietzsche. 2
vols. Edited by Erhart Thierbach. Weimar: Gesellschaft der Freunde des Nietzsche-Archivs, 1938 and
1940. This and the Gersdorff series are companion
volumes to the *Historisch-Kritische Gesamtausgabe,*
and have been done with the same scholarly care.
Wagner und Nietzsche zur Zeit ihrer Freundschaft. Edited
by Elisabeth Förster-Nietzsche. Munich: Georg Müller, 1915. In English: *The Nietzsche-Wagner Correspondence,* translated by Caroline Kerr. New York:
Boni and Liveright, 1922.
Much of the extensive correspondence between Nietzsche and Cosima and Richard Wagner was not preserved.

Also of some interest is *Friedrich Nietzsche und die
Frauen seiner Zeit.* Elisabeth Förster-Nietzsche. Mun-
ich: C. H. Beck, 1935. The second part, edited by Karl
Schlechta, contains some of Nietzsche's letters to Ma-
thilde Maier, Louise Ott, Sophie Ritschl, Meta von
Salis, Cosima Wagner, and others.

PART TWO: BIOGRAPHICAL SOURCES

Andler, Charles. *Nietzsche, sa Vie et sa Pensée.* 6 vols.
Paris: Bossard, 1920–1931. Vol. IV, *La Maturité de
Nietzsche,* is the most important of the volumes
biographically.
Andreas-Salomé, Lou. *Friedrich Nietzsche in seinen
Werken.* Vienna: Carl Konegen, 1894. Has illuminat-
ing sketches of Nietzsche.
_____ *Lebensrückblick,* edited by Ernst Pfeiffer. Frank-
furt a.M.: Insel, 1968. Pfeiffer's extensive notes, as
well as the text itself, shed much light on the char-
acters and relationships of Lou, Rée, and Nietzsche.
Note: the 1968 edition is a revised version of the 1951
(Zurich and Wiesbaden) edition.

Bernoulli, Carl Albrecht. *Franz Overbeck und Friedrich Nietzsche: eine Freundschaft.* 2 vols. Jena: Eugen Diederichs, 1908. An invaluable study; it was not unduly influenced by the Weimar Archive, and it contains many original biographical documents. This sprawling 1,000-page work has passages of biographical scholarship which are unsurpassed in the field.

Binion, Rudolph. *Frau Lou: Nietzsche's Wayward Disciple.* Princeton: Princeton University Press, 1968.

Blunck, Richard. *Friedrich Nietzsche: Kindheit und Jugend.* Munich and Basel: Ernst Reinhardt, 1953. A very thorough examination of the years before 1870.

Brandes, Georg. *Friedrich Nietzsche.* English translation from the Danish by A. G. Chater. London: Wm. Heinemann, 1914. This volume also contains the Nietzsche-Brandes correspondence.

Brann, Hellmut Walther. *Nietzsche und die Frauen.* Leipzig: Felix Meiner, 1931.

Deussen, Paul. *Erinnerungen an Friedrich Nietzsche.* Leipzig: F. A. Brockhaus, 1901.

Förster-Nietzsche, Elisabeth. *Das Leben Friedrich Nietzsches* 2 vols. Leipzig: C. G. Naumann, 1895–1904. Volume II is printed in two separate parts. Frequently referred to in German scholarship as "die grosse Biographie," to distinguish it from the following.

————— *Der junge Nietzsche.* Leipzig: Alfred Kröner, 1912; since 1925, vol. I of *Das Leben Friedrich Nietzsches, Kleine Ausgabe in zwei Bänden.*

————— *Der werdende Nietzsche.* Munich: Musarion, 1924.

————— *Der einsame Nietzsche.* Leipzig: Alfred Kröner, 1914; since 1925, vol. II of *Das Leben Friedrich Nietzsches, Kleine Ausgabe in zwei Bänden.*

Hildebrand, Kurt. *Gesundheit und Krankheit in Nietzsches Leben und Werk.* Berlin: S. Karger, 1926.

Hollingdale, R. J. *Nietzsche: The Man and His Philosophy.* Baton Rouge: Louisiana State University Press, 1965.

Jaspers, Karl. *Nietzsche: An Introduction to the Understanding of His Philosophical Activity.* Original German edition 1936. Translated by C. F. Wallraff and F. J. Schmitz. Tucson: University of Arizona Press, 1965. Book One focuses on Nietzsche's life.

Kaufmann, Walter. *Nietzsche: Philosopher, Psychologist, Antichrist.* 3rd edition, revised and enlarged. New York: Vintage, 1968; original version: Princeton University Press, 1950.

Meysenbug, Malwida von. *Gesammelte Werke.* 5 vols. Edited by Berta Schleicher. Stuttgart, Berlin, Leipzig: Deutsche Verlags-Anstalt, and Schuster and Loeffler, 1922). Volume III (*Gestalten*) contains an essay about Nietzsche.

Martin, Alfred von. *Nietzsche und Burckhardt.* Munich: Ernst Reinhardt, 1941.

Mittasch, Alwin, *Friedrich Nietzsches Naturbeflissenheit.* Heidelberg: Akademie der Wissenschaften, 1950. Documents Nietzsche's reading in, and correspondence about, the natural sciences and medicine, and his numerous consultations with specialists.

Oehler, Max. *Nietzsches Bibliothek.* Weimar: Gesellschaft der Freunde des Nietzsche-Archivs, 1942.

Overbeck, Franz. *Selbstbekenntnisse.* Edited by Eberhard Vischer. Basel: Benno Schwabe, 1941; new edition Frankfurt a.M.: Insel, 1966.

Podach, Erich. *Nietzsches Zusammenbruch.* Heidelberg: Niels Kampmann, 1930. English version: *The Madness of Nietzsche,* translated by F. Voigt. London, 1931. Podach's scholarship and objectivity place him with Andler and Bernoulli among the outstanding biographers of Nietzsche.

_____ *Gestalten um Nietzsche.* Weimar: Erich Lichtenstein, 1932. Includes discussions of Nietzsche's mother and sister, Förster, Gast, and Rohde.

_____ *Friedrich Nietzsche und Lou Salomé: Ihre Begegnung 1882.* Zurich and Leipzig: Max Niehans, 1938.

_____ *Friedrich Nietzsches Werke des Zusammenbruchs.* Heidelberg: Wolfgang Rothe, 1961. The appendix to this volume traces illuminating cross-references between Nietzsche's letters and books in his last active period.

Rohde, Erwin. *Afterphilologie: zur Beleuchtung des . . . Pamphlets "Zukunftsphilologie!" Sendschreiben eines Philologen an Richard Wagner.* Leipzig: E. W. Fritzsch, 1872.

Salin, Edgar. *Jacob Burckhardt und Nietzsche.* 2nd, expanded edition. Heidelberg: Lambert Schneider, 1948.

Salis-Marschlins, Meta von. *Philosoph und Edelmensch: ein Beitrag zur Charakteristik Friedrich Nietzsches.* Leipzig: C. G. Naumann, 1897.

Schlechta, Karl. *Der Fall Nietzsche: Aufsätze und Vorträge.* Munich: Carl Hanser, 1958.

Schleicher, Berta. *Malwida von Meysenbug: Ein Lebensbild.* 3rd edition. Berlin: Schuster and Loeffler, 1916.

Stroux, Johannes. *Nietzsches Professur in Basel.* Jena: Fromann, 1925.

Vinant, Gaby. *Malwida von Meysenbug: sa Vie et ses Amis.* Paris: Honoré Champion, 1932.

Wilamowitz-Möllendorff, Ulrich von. *Zukunftsphilologie! Eine Erwiderung auf Friedrich Nietzsches "Geburt der Tragödie."* 2 parts. Berlin: Gebrüder Borntraeger, 1872, 1873.

Note: Readers wishing further bibliographical information should consult the *International Nietzsche Bibliography,* compiled and edited by Herbert W. Reichert and Karl Schlechta (Chapel Hill: Univ. of North Carolina Press, 1960). This 133-page document contains entries in twenty-six languages, including Bulgarian, Icelandic, Serbian, and Vietnamese, although it does not claim to be complete. Each item is briefly described. No works *by* Nietzsche are listed.

Index of Recipients

Reference is to the page number on which the letter begins.

Reference is to page numbers. Persons listed in the Index of Recipients do not reappear below unless specifically referred to in the text.